Samhain

A Comprehensive Guide to Celebrating the New Year and Halloween, the Day of the Dead
(Wheel of the Year Series)

Laura Garcia

© **Copyright 2023 - All rights reserved.**

The content contained within this book may not be reproduced, duplicated or transmitted without direct written permission from the author or the publisher.

Under no circumstances will any blame or legal responsibility be held against the publisher, or author, for any damages, reparation, or monetary loss due to the information contained within this book, either directly or indirectly.

Legal Notice:

This book is copyright protected. It is only for personal use. You cannot amend, distribute, sell, use, quote or paraphrase any part, or the content within this book, without the consent of the author or publisher.

Disclaimer Notice:

Please note the information contained within this document is for educational and entertainment purposes only. All effort has been executed to present accurate, up to date, reliable, complete information. No warranties of any kind are declared or implied. Readers acknowledge that the author is not engaged in the rendering of legal, financial, medical or professional advice. The content within this book has been derived from various sources. Please consult a licensed professional before attempting any techniques outlined in this book.

By reading this document, the reader agrees that under no circumstances is the author responsible for any losses, direct or indirect, that are incurred as a result of the use of the information contained within this document, including, but not limited to, errors, omissions, or inaccuracies.

Table of Contents

Introduction 1

Chapter 1: Samhain for the Ordinary Person 9

Chapter 2: An Oak Enters a New Year 27

Chapter 3: New Year, New Testament 39

Chapter 4: Samhain Around the World 53

Chapter 5: Samhain Structures–Natural Materials 77

Chapter 6: Samhain Structures –The Altar 95

Chapter 7: Celebrating Samhain–Spells 109

Chapter 8: Celebrating Samhain–Rituals 125

Chapter 9: The Next Cycle 135

Conclusion	139
Thank You	143
About the Author	145
References	147

Introduction

Samhain therefore marks the beginning of darkness, and thus the beginning of life, a time for "The Gathering" of all beings. –Brendan Mac Gonagle

By their very nature, cycles must begin and they must end. Though the Gregorian calendar runs from January to December, there is another annual structure that is equally as important, albeit slightly less famous. This calendar also denotes an annum that begins on New Year's Day, one that is not tied to the months or the days as we know them, but rather the seasons. The focus of this book will be none other than this seasonal marker, the New Year's festival of Samhain.

Chances are you have heard of Samhain before, but associate it more closely with costumes, candy, and cornstarch-soaked slasher films. While the celebration of Halloween must not be discounted, its festivities are not our priority. Samhain is why we're here. This ancient and hallowed festival, one of the eight sabbats contained within the Wheel of the Year, is the reason this book exists. Given the importance of Samhain and festivals like it in cultures the world over, it can be difficult to know how to celebrate it, or even if one is allowed to host or participate in festivities. Naturally, the question of who may celebrate Samhain must be answered before any discussions of origins may be had, or plans for rituals may be made. Here enters the first bit of good news in this book: Samhain is open to all. The second bit of good news follows closely on the first's heels, as it is imperative to know that celebrating Samhain is extremely accessible, regardless of arbitrary characteristics such as ethnicity, background, sex or even beliefs. The beauty of festivals like Samhain is that there is a myriad of ways in which they may be appreciated and honored. Above all else, these festivals are malleable, and they may be integrated into a wide variety of worldviews and levels of ability. Moreover, appreciation and celebration of Samhain does not require any kind of exclusive belief. Many people from all walks of life celebrate Samhain, and a large number of them subscribe to an entirely different set of religious or spiritual beliefs.

So, whether you are looking to celebrate Samhain all on its own, want to incorporate it into the practices of your existing belief system, or simply wish to learn more about the sabbat, your purpose here is the same. Understanding the ins and outs of such an ancient festival can be tricky, and the sheer volume of differing interpretations can make it difficult to know where to begin when planning your festivities. This uncertainty can be overwhelming and ultimately discourage you from engaging with Samhain entirely. Feelings like these are entirely natural. Who among us hasn't opted out of doing something simply because we had no idea what was going on and figuring it out seemed to be entirely too complicated? If you find yourself in a situation like this when thinking of Samhain celebrations, rest assured that this book will guide you gently and comprehensively into the world of esoteric festivals.

The benefits of learning about Samhain stretch far beyond the acquisition of simple, theoretical knowledge. While understanding the tenets underlying the festival, its rites, and its rituals is important, gaining practical skills and an insight into the deeper meanings of Samhain celebrations is far more useful. That is what this book is for: to equip you with these skills, insights, and even the ability to create your own interpretation of Samhain. Throughout this book, you will find an array of rituals and practices, each of which is linked to the festival of the New Year. Pay close attention to the instructions that come with these descriptions, as their proper implementation will enable you to undertake the perfect Samhain celebration. Crucially, these instructions need not necessarily be followed to the letter. Remember the beautiful fluidity of these festivals. Each and every exercise, activity, spell, rite, and ritual can be adapted and customized to reflect the person who is celebrating Samhain, their values, and their beliefs more closely. It is very important to keep this in mind when working through this book and even afterwards as you prepare your chosen festivities. This book serves only as a guideline. Once you have finished reading it, the onus falls upon you to create your own version of Samhain, to take what you have learned and marry it with the things you already know and believe about the world and yourself. If everything goes well, what will result from this merger is a capacity within you to appreciate and celebrate the

Samhain sabbat (and any others of your choosing) on a deeper, more personal level.

Now, those of you who always preferred the written test to the practical, rest assured that you will not be left behind. It goes without saying that any type of practical execution requires a theoretical build-up. Rest assured that this book contains a considerable amount of information that is entirely theoretical. The fun of theory doesn't stop when the last chapter has been concluded, however, as the knowledge gained here will enable you to draw a line stretching from Samhain to Yule, through Litha and all the way to Mabon, completing the cycle. A big part of this book involves the establishment and maintenance of annual Samhain practices, and we can't very well let you go without making sure you understand how both this festival, as well as you yourself, fit into the greatest cycle of all, better known as the Wheel of the Year.

As you move through the contents of this book and deeper into the realm of spiritualism, what you will be doing is learning. Even if carrying out rites or invoking spells is not to your taste, there is still much to be gained from this book. If you look past the esoteric knowledge, discussions of Pagan beliefs, and tips on how to best honor the dead, you will find an undercurrent of affirmation and progression. If you turn the final page of this book and find yourself unconvinced that you can or should celebrate Samhain, take solace in the fact that while it may not have worked out the way you wanted, you still did something useful. By reading this book, regardless of its impact on you,

you are making progress in your spiritual journey. Perhaps you have never attempted to enrich your spiritual life before, and are just now taking your first steps. If that is the case, think of this book as a caregiver who is with you all the time, providing you with support and guidance as you begin navigating the spiritual world. Conversely, if you have been immersed in the world of esoteric knowledge for quite some time, regard this book as a supplement, perhaps even a type of spice, something used to add flavor or improve potency, rather than something meant to provide structure. Regardless of your level of spiritual insight and evolution, there is something you need in your life, and its pursuit has led you here.

Frankly speaking, this is the best place you can come to learn about Samhain, as I started in the same place you did. Everything I know about the sabbats and about spiritualism, I have learned through exploration and trial-and-error. That being said, I have been using these practices long enough to know what works, what doesn't, what should be thrown out, and what should be protected at all costs. My life is dedicated to the discovery, exploration, and expansion of this type of esoteric knowledge, and I have seen first-hand how embracing these types of rituals can impact and improve your spiritual health. Like I said, something led you here in the same way that something led me to the place where I first began my spiritual journey. If your purpose here is to learn, mine is to take you by the hand and tap into your heart, as I guide you along this journey. I have seen and felt so many beautiful things since I began my own journey, and I would love nothing more than to bring that same sense of revelatory beauty to your life now. If you're up for it, we can begin this new cycle, and find your place in it, together. What better starting point than Samhain?

Before we can dive into the practice of Samhain, it is important to understand the origins of this venerable, sacred sabbat. Samhain is celebrated over two days, beginning at sunset on October 31 and concluding at sunset the following day, November 1st. While etymology isn't exactly our main focus here, it is worth noting that the origin of the term *Samhain* is disputed. While many scholars maintain that it is a combination of the Celtic words *samh*, meaning summer, and *fuin,* meaning a conclusion or act of concealment, there are others which believe the festival's name has a much older origin (Mac Gonagle, 2016). The latter group argue that *Samhain* is derived from the Proto-Celtic word *samoni*, which denotes an assembly, or perhaps even the Gaulish *samonos* or *samonios*, both forms of which also refer to a gathering or reunion of some sort, with the original meaning of the root word *samoni* then being translated as describing a gathering of the living and the dead. Regardless of which argument you favor, it is clear that the original words used to describe Samhain encompassed the essence of the sabbat as it is observed to this day.

Given Samhain's presence on the Wheel of the Year, we know that it is a seasonal festival. More specifically, Samhain serves as a marker of the end of one season and the beginning of another. When Samhain is celebrated, both the harvest season, as well as summer, have come to an end, and it is time to move into winter, alongside which a new year is ushered in. Samhain has its roots in Celtic Paganism (more on that later), but has evolved over time to be celebrated by other spiritual and religious groups, each of which attach a different meaning to the festival. Original Samhain festivities involved walks in nature, the building of outdoor altars, as well as communing with deceased members of the community. Throughout all the different interpretations of the sabbat, there is one crucial element that remains: its tie to nature. Samhain is about the cycle of time and of life, neither of which would function as they do without the power of nature. As such, Samhain celebrations, whether they be Pagan, Christian or Druidic always center around nature. Samhain is a powerful festival, and however you interpret it or adapt its rituals, this power and the beauty thereof must always be respected, acknowledged, and celebrated.

CHAPTER 1:

Samhain for the Ordinary Person

> *Samhain is a time that humans have, for centuries, honored their dead, told fortunes, planned for the year ahead, and celebrated what they have achieved or reaped in the previous year.* –Kerry Ward

In the twenty-first century, observing Samhain has been revamped almost entirely to suit the sensibilities of modern celebrants. Rituals have changed and evolved, spells have become increasingly more contemporary, and gatherings have been adapted to accommodate a more modern, cosmopolitan set of attendees. That being said, the roots of Samhain have not been forgotten. In fact, the modern trimmings introduced into Samhain festivities are all attached to the structure of the original Pagan sabbat. In this chapter, we will explore the pre-Christian origins of Samhain and examine how both the major tenets of the festival, as well as the celebrations used for its observance have changed through the centuries.

The New Year, Peasants, and the Dead

Today, if you mention the name Samhain, the first thing that springs to mind is communing with a person's ancestors and engaging with the world of the deceased. While this does form an important part of the sabbat, celebrating Samhain as a Day of the Dead was not a fixture in early Pagan tradition.

In Ancient Celtic culture, Samhain was celebrated purely as a seasonal festival, forming one of the four major fire festivals, each denoting a change in the seasons, and subsequently in the practice of agriculture. For the Ancient Celts, Samhain marked the end of summer, serving as an official end to the harvest festival and ushering in a new year. With the different fire festivals each marking the beginning of a new season, Samhain served as the first of the four festivals which would take place throughout the year. Oftentimes, Samhain is regarded as marking the entrance of the people into the 'dark' part of the year. In the time of the Ancient Celts, this darkness was linked to an array of things, among them a number of 'dark' deities such as Cailleach (also known as the Hag or the Winter Crone), Donn (the god of the dead), and even Crom Crúaich, a deity most famous for his rather strong connection to ritual sacrifice (Mac Gonagle, 2016). Today, this darkness is associated with the Day of the Dead aspect of Samhain (more on that in a moment), when it was originally intended to signify the coming of winter, during which the days are shorter and the nights longer, meaning that there is more "darkness" in the year than there was before. While modern-day interpretations like these are not incorrect, they are significantly more poetic than the way in which Ancient Celtic Pagans viewed Samhain. The festival was extremely functional, as it was used to turn the page on the calendar and signal to the community that it was time to start a new farming cycle. If you aren't already convinced of how closely Samhain is tied to the seasonal cycle, consider the fact that Pagans chose the end of October for this festival because it falls exactly at the midpoint between Mabon (better known as the fall equinox) and Yule (though Christmassy in name, Yule is in fact the winter solstice).

To their credit, Pagans did not only view Samhain as a perfunctory festival of demarcation. In actuality, they attached a great deal of meaning and sentiment to the sabbat. To start, Samhain was celebrated as a fire festival, similar to each of the three other seasonal festivals. The reason why Ancient Celtic Pagans involved fire so heavily in their holidays is that they believed the flames to be capable of great acts of cleansing and protection. Samhain festivities always kicked off with a big bonfire built and lit in the village. The kindling for the bonfire was usually arranged in the shape of a wheel, and while the exact meaning of this is debated, we can assume that the circular wheel was chosen because of the shape's prominence in sacred geometry, because it was thought to resemble the sun, a celestial body tied closely to life, or because the structure would be seen as symbolic of the

Wheel of the Year. Given the celebration of Samhain as the beginning of a new year, the latter seems more likely, with the Pagans perhaps metaphorically lighting the previous year on fire to cleanse community members of the preceding year. Crucially, the bonfire had to be ignited through friction (i.e. the striking of flint rocks against one another or the rubbing together of sticks in order to make a flame), as Ancient Celts firmly believed that they could only be cleansed and protected through what they called a 'friction fire' (Foley & O'Donnell, 2009). By starting one of these fires, they could protect not only themselves, but also their livestock and crops from dangers such as infestation, plague, and even the perils of witchcraft. The protection of the flames was not reserved for the great outdoors, with Pagans keeping their hearth fires lit using flaming branches that had been set alight by the great bonfire. Every night of Samhain, after attending communal festivities, each family in the community had to take a piece of the fire with them. Upon returning home, they were meant to douse the existing hearth fire and light a new one using the bonfire flame. Not only did this mean that their homes and their inhabitants were protected, but the use of the communal bonfire was a powerful bonding force among members of different villages. Each of them had used the same flame, each of them fell under the same protection, and so each of them could enter the new year as members of a unified and connected cohort.

Samhain was an incredibly important festival in Ancient Celtic culture, so much so that attendance of its festivities was non-negotiable. If you weren't a participant in the celebrations, you were one of two things: an organizer or dead. There was no in-between. In fact, if you used your own death as an excuse to miss Samhain, there was an excellent chance that you had skipped out on some festivities before and that your demise was justice handed down by the gods. That being said, if you were one of the gods' favorites, you might have gotten off light, being punished with a simple, severe illness. If there was any doubt before about the importance of Samhain to the Ancient Celts, let there be no doubt anymore.

The seriousness of Samhain pervaded so many aspects of Ancient Celtic culture that even the military was involved in the celebrations. In Irish celebrations of Samhain, members of the community were made to present themselves to local chieftains and regional kings. Alongside these prominent figures sat the leaders of their military forces, usually on special Samhain thrones which had been constructed specifically for them (Brown, 2022). While these displays of fealty had little to do with agriculture, the change of seasons, or the start of the new year, it can be argued that these particular rituals were meant to serve as a method of unification, similar to the lighting of the hearth fires with bonfire flames. Kings, chiefs, politicians, and generals asked their people to gather in front of them in order to reaffirm their loyalty to the community and its prosperity. Keep in mind that this prosperity could range from helping plant the crops and harvesting them later in the year, to enlisting in the military and fighting incumbent forces if war ever broke out.

Though we may be surprised by the presence of the military at what appears to be a peaceful, agricultural festival, their presence is what brought the peace. During celebrations of Samhain, all conflict was brought to a halt. Clans that were feuding laid down their arms, neighbors locked in dispute over a particularly healthy cow pressed pause, and even domestic disagreements were set aside for the new year. In fact, in many of the Ancient Celtic clans, anyone found to be engaged in any type of conflict, or who made use of any type of weapon would be liable to pay a hefty fine (History.com Editors, 2018a). Given that the beginning of another year is traditionally a time for renewal, a hiatus from conflict provided the people with a chance for a clean slate, entering the new year with calm and peace of mind, leaving behind the weight of disagreement in the cycle that passed.

Because Samhain is nothing if not versatile, another important aspect of the festival's celebrations involved food. Though Samhain officially lasted only a day, perhaps two, some Ancient Celtic groups took to extending the festival to as many as six days. On each of these days, they would hold great feasts and consume an ungodly quantity of alcohol. Once their crops, livestock, homes, and children had been cleansed, there was no reason why they couldn't get a bit rowdy to ring in the new year. Although many modern minds would like to believe that society has evolved far beyond the primitive customs of our forebears, there is an element of this ancient hedonism that remains prominent in present day New Year's festivities.

It is clear to see that a number of celebrations of the Samhain sabbat were geared towards including the entire community. While these larger festivities were aimed at unifying towns, villages, and clans, smaller rites also formed part of Samhain. These rituals, ordinarily performed in the privacy of the family home, were also rituals of bonding. However, instead of bringing together hundreds of residents of a small hamlet, these rituals served to unite the few people that made up a family.

These practices are those that originated the practice of observing the Samhain sabbat. While these festivities may not exist now in exactly the same form they did back then, their establishment laid the foundation for all Samhain celebrations that have followed in the centuries since the first festive bonfire was lit.

Samhain in the New Millennium

Very few things in life ever stay the same, even ancient festivals. As time has worn on and the beliefs and spiritual practices of the general populace have changed, so have the rites and rituals associated with the festival of Samhain. Before we examine how exactly these festivities have changed, it is important to remember that Samhain has simply evolved, and that those aspects of the festival which make up its foundation have largely remained the same millennia later.

The first, and perhaps most significant, way in which Samhain has changed over the time is the expansion of the meaning of the festival to include honoring the dead. As already indicated, Samhain was originally only a festival season, one intended to mark the ending of one cycle and the beginning of another. Nowadays, however, Samhain is more closely associated with the machinations of the world of the hereafter than with the agricultural calendar of the living. That being said, while many of the aspects of the modern-day Halloween were associated with Samhain only after the advent of Christianity, the Ancient Celtic festival was not entirely unconnected to the land of the deceased (Kolirin, 2022). Ancient Celts really did believe that the veil between this world and the next was thin. Though this belief was not always as connected to Samhain as it is nowadays, the Ancient Celts did adopt a celebration of the dead as part of their year-end festivities.

In the pre-Christian era, Celtic Pagans believed that spirits would enter the world of the living once the doors to the hereafter had opened. Once these doors were ajar, the Pagans had several rituals in place that they could use in order to commune with and honor the spirits of those they knew who had passed on. The most well-known of these rituals is that of the 'dumb supper.' In this case, the usage of the word 'dumb' relates not to intelligence, but to noise (Kolirin, 2022). Dumb suppers are meant to be eaten in total silence, the lack of idle conversation intended as a signal of respect to the souls of those who have passed on. Dumb suppers are also not your average meal, as they are eaten in reverse. Ancient Celtic culture maintained a strong link between the world of the dead, also known as the Otherworld, and doing things in reverse. By starting their meals with dessert, Pagans felt that they were able to connect with the Otherworld through this reversal. They then strengthened this connection by setting a place for the deceased persons being celebrated. The meal was then eaten in complete silence, with attendees often encouraged to think of the invited departed and their time on Earth. Upon the conclusion of the meal, a bell was rung and the silence broken. After the ringing of the bell, conversations resumed and the meal could be transformed into a party, bringing it more closely in line with the spirit of the original Samhain. Dumb suppers have mostly stood the test of time, with many modern Pagans choosing to celebrate the lives and deaths of their loved ones through these silent meals.

Another ancient custom which has endured is that of Mari Lwyd. Meaning 'white mare' in Welsh, this ritual originated in the Southern parts of Wales, and became incorporated into Samhain festivities over time. This ritual is significantly more modern than some of the others performed at Samhain, as it is believed that Mari Lwyd was first performed in the latter half of the 19th century (Kolirin, 2022). At the time, the reception of the ritual was not all that great, and its use in Samhain festivals soon died out. Now, however, the white mare is making a comeback. During Samhain festivals, a horse skull is attached to the top of a pole, over which a white sheet is draped. This mechanical mare is then carried throughout town by a group of followers, one of whom is known as the 'Ostler,' and who speaks for the creature. They stop at each door, demanding entry. The followers and the inhabitants of the building then have an exchange, one which Mari Lwyd wins, and then the group outside is offered food and drink. This offer is transactional, however, as Mari Lwyd is expected to bless each person who lives there as they enter the new year. Mari Lwyd is an appropriate addition to the canon of Samhain, as the horse effigy is as versatile as the festival itself. Not only is she seen as a vessel of blessing, but she is also said to embody various spirits, more specifically those of mischief and chaos. In addition to this, Mari Lwyd is also the guardian of the dark half of the year, with her blessings allowing people entry into it. Finally, Mari Lwyd adds to her already robust workload by acting as a sort of Pagan Ferryman, transporting the souls of the deceased from this world to the next. As I said, versatile.

Other rituals that modern observers have maintained are those of the symbolic bonfire. In the past, each village would light a communal bonfire as the center of their Samhain festivities. Nowadays, given the esoteric nature of Pagan Samhain, there are dedicated fire festivals which provide such a bonfire for visitors from all over. The most well-known of these modern fire festivals takes place in the city of Edinburgh in the United Kingdom, and is known as the Samhuinn Fire Festival (Kolirin, 2022). The UK remains the epicenter of Samhain festivities, as another popular Samhain celebration takes place annually in the city of Cornwall. There, at the Museum of Witchcraft and Magic, the Dark

Gathering is held every year on Samhain. The Dark Gathering is essentially another fire festival, albeit one that combines both the original, seasonal version of Samhain and the newer, Day of the Dead incarnation. The festival hosts Morris Dancers, groups traditionally associated with the changing of seasons, as well as a variety of rituals meant to commune with and venerate the ancestors of its attendees. Regardless of the specifics, both the Edinburgh and Cornwall festivals remain true to the original style of Samhain, as both events are massive celebrations with music, dancing, and most importantly, copious amounts of alcohol.

These festivities are open to everyone, and are often attended both by people who firmly believe in the power of Samhain, as well as those for whom the fire, dancing, and pageantry are merely a casual sort of novelty. In the former group, we often find Wiccans and Neo-Pagans. Before we dive into the modernization of Samhain by these groups, it is important to understand the following: Wicca is regarded as a religion which evolved from the practices and beliefs of ancient Pagans (Foley & O'Donnell, 2009). As such, for the purposes of simplification, we will refer to both groups as 'Neo-Pagans' for the remainder of this book. While there are certain differences in core beliefs between the two groups, when it comes to Samhain, their rites and rituals are strikingly similar. More importantly, most of their Samhain celebrations stay close to those practiced by the Pagans of pre-Christian time. It is significant, however, to note that Neo-Pagans do not carry their name simply because they are Pagans in the New Age. Rather, it has to do with the fact that they have found new and different ways in which to practice their beliefs, ones that are more appropriate for today's age, and that opened the door for people from all walks of life to join in the celebration.

In effect, what Neo-Pagans have done with Samhain is take the parts built by the Ancient Celtic Pagans which they feel are most suited to their purposes and tailored them to fit modern Paganism (Foley & O'Donnell, 2009). This is important, as this change allowed those who wanted to celebrate Samhain or transform the rituals in different ways to go down their chosen path. We see this in the dates on which Neo-Pagans celebrate Samhain. While the majority do prescribe to the notion that Samhain serves as a marker of the new year, it is not everyone who chooses to celebrate this occasion beginning at sunset on October 31st. A more flexible approach is taken, with many of the adherents to Neo-Paganism forming subgroups which then celebrate the sabbat on another day, usually one that is more convenient for or meaningful to the members of the group.

Continuing with the theme of Neo-Pagan reinterpretation, we look at the 'darkness' that is heralded by the arrival of Samhain. For older groups, this darkness was many things, but above all else it was indicative of the coming winter. For many Neo-Pagans, the darkness still represents the beginning of the colder months. However, they go a step further and use this darkness as an opportunity to turn to the darkness within.

During celebrations of Samhain, many Neo-Pagans engage in introspection, examining the complex emotional issues they may be facing and make an attempt to resolve these problems (Foley & O'Donnell, 2009). This resolution (or at the very least the attempting thereof) is meant to be a type of cleansing ritual. In the same way that older generations stopped conflict on the eve of the new year, so do Neo-Pagans attempt to leave their own, inner conflict in the cycle that expires.

Neo-Pagans have adapted Samhain's darkness in another, more significant way. In the 21st century, Samhain is celebrated entirely as both the coming of the new year, as well as the festival of the dead. Neo-Pagans are of the belief that Samhain is the perfect time to honor the dead, and as such, they commune with spirits and invite them to join the living in their Samhain rituals. Interestingly, the belief that the veil between worlds thins at Samhain does not restrict its effects only to interacting with the dead. During this time, it is said that providence is able to operate more thoroughly, as the thinning of the veil allows people to gain supernatural knowledge, specifically as it pertains to events yet to come. This belief is taken to heart by Neo-Pagans, who engage in divinatory practices during Samhain through means of scrying mirrors and crystal balls. Neo-Pagans extend the effects of the thinned veil even further, postulating that it is not only the spirits of the dead that cross over during this time, but all manner of supernatural creatures, especially fairies (Foley & O'Donnell, 2009). As such, many Neo-Pagans have adopted rituals that honor these creatures and made them a part of their personal Samhain festivities. To their credit, this belief is one that Neo-Pagans have inherited from their pre-Christian forebears, as many Ancient Celtic Pagans were known to also believe in the crossing over of more than just spirits. There is a significant difference, however, in the way in which fairies are viewed by each of the two groups. Where the rites of Neo-Pagans are intended to honor the fairies and celebrate them, the Ancient Celtic Pagans were fearful of them, often performing Samhain rituals involving metals like iron, which they believed capable of warding off or injuring the entities–yet another example of evolution and modernization.

These are not the only rituals which Neo-Pagans have decided to preserve as part of their celebrations. Every Samhain, Neo-Pagans still build altars, hold seasonal feasts, and engage in a variety of outdoor rituals, each aimed at replicating the practices of those who came before them. The only differences are that the altars are built on tables or mantles, not stone hearths, the feasts often involve modern cuisine, and the outdoor rituals take place in backyards or parks, not great Irish forests. In other words, things have been made more modern.

While this is all extremely fascinating, it does beg the question of how exactly Samhain came to function as a sort of Pagan Day of the Dead. The answer is actually quite simple: modernization and the spread of ideas. Over the centuries, as European forces ventured out into the world and conquered different parts of the globe, an exchange of ideas and customs occurred between the invading forces and the inhabitants of each respective land. When Christians arrived in Ireland, where the Pagan, Celtic Samhain was being celebrated, they learned about the festival and began to utilize its most basic aspects in order to spread the message of their own belief system. While Christianity and Samhain will be discussed more in-depth in a later chapter, it is important to know now that it was through the appropriation of the Samhain customs by Christian forces that All Hallow's Eve, and All Saints' Day were established in addition to All Souls' Day, a day which would eventually evolve to become the Halloween that is celebrated to this day. Though initially the Pagan Samhain and the Christian All Hallow's Eve existed as entirely separate entities, as the centuries went by and Paganism faded into obscurity, the lines between the two blurred, resulting in the mixture of seasonal festival and Day of the Dead we know today as Halloween.

By all appearances, modern Pagan celebrations have remained true to the spirit of the original Ancient Celtic festivals of Samhain, for the most part. Over time, components have been added and taken away, and the definition of Samhain has been somewhat expanded. Regardless of any changes made, at its core, Samhain is still a celebration of cycles, of beginnings and endings, and of transition, whether from the light part of the year to the dark, or from life to death. Either way, Samhain is still the beautiful, lively festival it has always been.

Key Takeaways

- The festival of Samhain has roots in the culture of the Ancient, pre-Christian Celtic civilization.

- Originally, the festival was celebrated by Pagans, and served only to mark the end of the year and the harvest season, but over time, it came to include the honoring and celebrating of deceased members of the community.

- In later centuries, after the arrival of Christianity in Ireland, Samhain was expanded to include the celebration of the dead.

- Samhain is the first of four seasonal fire festivals, as determined by the Wheel of the Year.

- The use of fire in Samhain is intended as a method of cleansing and protecting, allowing observers to enter the new year with a clean slate.

- Traditionally, Samhain is a time for peace, and all conflict must be put aside during the festival.

- The celebration of Samhain has endured through the centuries, and there are still fire festivals being held today.

- In the 21st century, Neo-Pagans who celebrate Samhain have changed some of the traditions of the sabbat, while doing away entirely with some of the others.

- Any and all changes made to the way in which Samhain is celebrated is intended only to open up the festivities to more people, and to allow everyone who wants to participate to adapt the rites and rituals to suit them better.

CHAPTER 2:

An Oak Enters a New Year

> [T]hey ended up presenting the Romans with many peculiarities...which generated a certain fear and curiosity, mainly on the part of the Druids. –André Luiz de Souza Soares

Druids and the Night of the Thin Veil

Much like the festival of Samhain itself, Druidry finds its origin in the beliefs and practices of the Ancient Celtic people. In fact, Druids formed an important part of Ancient Celtic culture, and performed a number of roles in the community. They worked in the field of justice, acting as members of a jury during trials. Additionally, they poured their efforts and knowledge into the finer, more abstract things such as music and thinking. Druids were healers for the communities in which they lived. Most importantly, however, was their functioning as the religious leaders of the Ancient Celtic people (De Souza Soares, 2013). Essentially, the Druids would act in the same capacity as the priests known today and are often described using the same word. It is crucial, however, to make a distinction between Druidry and Paganism. While Druids did act as sort-of priests for the Ancient Celts, who practice Paganism, the Druids themselves adhered to a different set of beliefs. Though Paganism was similarly influenced by nature, the importance of the natural world was emphasized much more greatly in the Druidic faith. Druidic worship of nature went hand-in-hand with a love for creativity. Thus, Druids were educated in such a way that they could strike a balance between their devotion to nature and the development of their creative faculties.

When it came to Samhain, however, ancient Druids set down the paint brushes and chisels and stepped into the shoes of the ceremony master. Cast your mind back to the first chapter, where we learned about the bonfire of Samhain, the one whose importance stretches across nearly the entire sabbat. At the end of the last harvest day of the season, the day on which Samhain began, members of the community would congregate for the lighting of the bonfire. When they came to the place where the kindling had been laid, who would they find holding the torch meant to ignite it all? None other than a druid. In their capacity as priests, the Druids would light the fire of Samhain and officially begin the festival. Here we see the overlap of the Druidic and Pagan celebrations of Samhain (De Souza

Soares, 2013). This should come as no surprise, given the meaning attached to the fire. The very presence of the fire is ritualistic and spiritual, and its purpose is to cleanse all those who participate in the ritual of its burning. While we would call this supernatural today, for the Pagans and Druids of the time, it was simply supernatural (cheesy, I'm aware, but the point comes across). While the Druids and Pagans have the bonfire in common, the Druids made use of it in a way the others did not. During the sabbat, Druids would gather around the fire in a circle, each holding the skulls of their ancestors. This ritual was meant to provide protection to their entire community. Given their dedication to the esoteric nature of each of the natural elements, it makes sense entirely for Druids to play such a significant role in the most prominent and occult of the Samhain festivities.

As we already know, Samhain was originally a harvest festival, with the connotations of death being added to the mix in later centuries (Bhagat, 2018). Interestingly, however, is the fact that the Ancient Celts did believe in a thinning of the veil between two worlds. While they did not necessarily connect this thinning to the Otherworld, they did believe that supernatural creatures and deities could cross over into our world more easily on the night of Samhain. These creatures included witches, fairies, and all manner of spirits covering the entire spectrum between benevolence and evil. In Ireland, a connection was made between Samhain and the appearance of fairies, as these creatures were viewed as deities of growth. Remember that Samhain is not only a celebration of the harvest reaped in the old year, but also an appeal for blessings for the harvest to come in the new year. As such, growth deities like fairies were honored on this night as a means of spiritual preparation for the agricultural cycle to come. This providence was important, largely because the winter (which began on the night of Samhain) was regarded as one of the evils entering the world. In the winter, no crops were planted or harvested, and if food supplies ran short, the chances for recovering the lost resources were very small. The fairies were presented as the good force opposing this seasonal evil. Another important, supernatural figure in Druidic celebrations of Samhain is that of Cailleach, also known as the Crone. Druids have long believed that Cailleach is responsible for the turn of the seasons during the sabbat, stating that she uses her abilities to strip the trees of their leaves. In doing so, the Druids say, she speeds up the death of the old year, and germinates the seed that will blossom into a new one (*Samhain*, n.d). The Crone is honored in ways similar to those of the fairies, as it is thought that she can provide people with clean slates and take away their troubles and sorrows in the present so that they may have a better, more beautiful future. In essence, Cailleach brings about the death of the old year with all its baggage. We see this line of thinking carrying through to the association of death with Samhain later on. Samhain festivities include celebrations of life in order to combat the evil sadness of death, and in some beliefs, even the evil forces which bring about death and carry souls to the other world.

While Druids performed other rituals throughout the entire year, those performed at) Samhain were regarded as especially potent. This is because of the high regard in which Druids held borders. Liminality was incredibly important to pre-Christian Druids, and times and spaces that were 'in-between' were thought to be holy (OBOD, 2019). Physical transitive spaces, also known as 'border places,' were things such as shores, bridges and borders between communities, towns, and countries. There were more abstract spaces thought to be holy as well, specifically temporal ones. For instance, many rites were performed at dawn or dusk, when the world was in between day and night. Samhain was one of these holy times, marking the liminal seasonal space between winter and summer (ancient Druids and Pagans recognized only these two seasons). During Samhain, when the thinning of the veil and the change of seasons came together, Druids believed that time lost all meaning. Essentially, the past, present, and future all became one. It is because of this that we see the celebration of the year gone by, as well as the divination of the year that lies ahead.

Similar to their Pagan counterparts, Druids would host dumb suppers. In the Druidic tradition, the place that was set for the deceased was at the head of the table. While attendees ate their supper in silence, they also refrained from looking at the space designated for spirits. Druids believed that it was extremely bad luck to look at the deceased. After the ritual meal was finished, the cup and plate would be taken from this place and put in the woods for use by the pookas, another type of supernatural Celtic creature (OBOD, 2019). In addition to these dumb suppers, Druids would also celebrate Samhain through the telling of ghost stories, a tradition which has endured all the way through to modern celebrations of Halloween. Druids also engaged in fortune telling during Samhain, and people who possessed the Second Sight found themselves to be particularly popular on the night of the sabbat. Finally, Druids would also celebrate Samhain by forming groves. These groves are ritual circles, and could be used for a number of purposes (De Souza Soares, 2013). Druids would form these circles and give thanks for the harvest of the year, honor the lives of those who had passed, and appeal to the deities for blessings for themselves and the community in the new year.

Neo-Druids and Samhain

Druidic practice is intrinsically tied to Samhain, as well as to several other sabbats. In ancient times, the knowledge of this esoteric group was reserved for select members of the community. Over time, however, those who hold this knowledge grew in number, and with this growth came the evolution of the

Druids' Samhain, which in turn evolved into the more personal, more accessible celebrations that are hosted today. As with ancient Druidry, we must determine what exactly Neo-Druidry is before we can talk about the beliefs and rituals of its adherents.

Neo-Druidry is the evolution of the original practice that originated with the Ancient Celts (Bishop, 2019). In fact, Neo-Druidry can be seen as a sort of resurrection of the Druidic practice. While the beliefs and rituals of the Druids never died out entirely, they remained obscured and essentially dormant for many centuries. Then, in the 20th century, life was breathed into the ruins of the ancient groves. From this restorative breath sprung a group of people who sought to practice a form of spiritualism, and wished to continue on the traditions and practices of those revered Ancient Celtic priests. Neo-Druidry, also known as Neo-Pagan Druidry, is in fact not one single set of beliefs, but rather an entire constellation of religious practices and philosophies, each of which find their origin in the Druids of centuries before. Neo-Druids are often pantheists who view God as part of a larger, interconnected system that also includes nature and the human body. According to the Neo-Druidic school of thought, nature is a sacred and benevolent entity, one which is connected to everything on Earth. Certain aspects of nature, such as animals, are thought to be able to bestow gifts on Druids (Bishop, 2019). These gifts include those of divination, healing, and knowledge, among others. While many of those who adhere to the Neo-Druidic belief approach their practice through a polytheistic lens, many modern Druids prefer a duotheistic outlook, and some even go the traditional route and adhere to monotheism.

Neo-Druids share an important point of view with their Celtic predecessors: the Otherworld. As we know, Ancient Celtic Druids thought of the Otherworld as the place found after death, where all souls must go upon leaving their human vessels. While Neo-Druids share this belief in the Otherworld and its function as a collecting place for the dead, they also believe that access to it is not attainable only after death (Bishop, 2019). Rather, Neo-Druids employ rituals such as meditation, dreaming, hypnosis, or the entering of trance states to visit this realm while they still live. This is important for our understanding of their celebration of Samhain, as Neo-Druids undertake these rituals during the sabbat, believing it to be easier to reach the Otherworld on the night the veil is thinned.

What is most important for us to understand about the religion of Neo-Druidry is the diversity that underlies each aspect of its practice. Underlying this modern belief system is an inherent sense of freedom. Modern Druids do not have or use specific, commonly known prayers or invocations, nor do they require adherents to perform any specific type of ritual. Rather, Neo-Druidic practitioners are encouraged to take their beliefs and celebrate them in the way that feels right for the individual (Bishop, 2019). This means that while the vast majority of modern Druids make use of evolved versions of religious teachings and practices, they are free to observe ancient customs. It must be said, however, that such ritual offerings would not go over well with other members of your grove, so it might be wise to stick to the wonders of nature and the philosophies that arise from them. While modern teachings encourage Druids to venture forth and create their own path, there are still a number of rites which have been inherited from the Ancient Celts. One such ritual is the congregation of the Druids in a sacred circle, the shape of which is meant to symbolize and promote unity among those in attendance. While in these circles, various chants are made, and blessings are bestowed upon attendees with water, and importantly, fire.

It may be difficult to see exactly how Neo-Druids celebrate Samhain, but that is only because of the diversity of their festivities. Many modern Druids choose to attend fire festivals, while others may participate in the skull circle ceremony. What's important for Neo-Druidic Samhain celebrations is the presence of the people in nature (Bishop, 2019). Both the sabbat and the Druids have incredibly deep connections to the natural world. Regardless of the choice of festivity, as long as those participating in the event feel some connection to the natural world, and perhaps even the supernatural world at the peak of Samhain, they are doing it right. They may feel this connection during moonlit walks, dumb suppers, bonfire festivals, Morris dances, or through participation in a sacred circle. As long as they feel it, and as long as it suits their wants, needs, and intentions, they can consider their Samhain celebration a success.

Key Takeaways

- While Ancient Celtic Druids formed part of the Pagan celebrations of Samhain, they held a separate set of beliefs and practiced a separate set of rituals.

- During the sabbat, Ancient Celtic Druids made sure that the balance between good and evil, between this world and the next was maintained.

- In the Druidic religion, in-between places and times are sacred, and as such, Samhain is an incredibly important and powerful time for Druids.

- Both ancient and modern Druids believe in the existence of the Otherworld, the place where souls go once they have left the body of a person.

- Modern Druids are known as Neo-Druids, and have evolved the practice to be much more diverse and accessible in terms of teachings and rituals.

- Neo-Druids are encouraged to find their own way in which to celebrate Samhain, but are still welcome to partake in established traditions such as dumb suppers and sacred circles.

- In both ancient and modern Druidic celebrations of Samhain, the most important thing is to commune with the world around you, as well as the one beyond.

CHAPTER 3:
New Year, New Testament

> *Samhain's equivalent on the Christian calendar is All Saints' Day, introduced by the Catholic church partly to supplant the Pagan festival of the dead.* –Bettina Arnold

Throughout the entirety of human existence, things have been able to coexist. Whether natural or manmade, most things on Earth have been able to live alongside one another, and while some of these parallel existences have been undertaken begrudgingly, for the most part they have gone off without a hitch. However, because nothing in this world is perfect, not everything demonstrates this propensity for coexistence. In cases like these, the two opposites, whether human, animal, or abstract, may find themselves experiencing some friction. In this chapter, we will examine how the festival of Samhain was viewed by the early Christian church, and how leaders of the church adopted and changed the festival's customs in order to bring its celebrants closer to the state of Christendom that church leaders envisioned.

The Church and Halloween

Centuries ago, Christian missionaries set out from Rome and journeyed to all corners of the Earth, hoping to spread their gospel to the people they encountered in their travels. The church was hopeful that the message of the Lord would be spread as far as possible, so groups of missionaries were formed and sent out into the world, one such group being dispatched to meet and Christianize the Ancient Celtic people. More specifically, they were sent to preach their teachings to the Ancient Celtic people of Ireland. Records show that the first Christians arrived on Irish soil in 431 AD at the behest of Pope Celestine I (De Souza Soares, 2013). The most prominent of these missionaries was Bishop Palladius, who would become one of the most famous figures in the history of Irish Catholicism, alongside Saint Patrick.

In the 5th century, the Christian missionaries went to work, their directive still fresh in their minds. As envoys of the Catholic Church of Rome, a religious body entirely foreign to the Ancient Celts, their earliest efforts of evangelism did not work out exactly the way they had hoped. Consequently, in 601 AD, Pope Gregory I issued an edict concerning the Christianization of native tribes across the globe. In his order, the pope instructed missionaries to adopt a gentler, more integrative approach (De Souza Soares, 2013). Where they had previously attempted to replace the native peoples' customs with those of Christianity in their entirety, the papal dispatch now instructed them to take what was already there and simply make it Christian. What this boils down to is that the missionaries were instructed to strip away the meanings attached to the rites, rituals, and religious symbols of the Ancient Celtic people (in the case of the Irish Celts, their Pagan religious practices) and replace them with new, Christian significance. Instead of tearing down altars or places of worship, missionaries repurposed them for the observance of Christianity.

Naturally, what's most important to us is the way in which the Catholic Church rebranded Pagan festivals, and luckily, their rebuilding of Samhain is one of the most famous examples of religious reconstruction. Because the church could not scrap Samhain entirely and replace it with a Christian festival, they instead recontextualized the former harvest festival. They began by finding the thing that both Paganism and Christianity had in common: a fervent belief in the supernatural (Kiger, 2020). For Ancient Celtic Pagans, the supernatural manifested itself in the form of spirits, fairies, witches, and creatures. For Catholics, the supernatural made its appearance in the works and deeds of their saints, specifically in the miracles which they were said to have performed. Using this as a jumping-off point, the Catholic Church took possession of the first day of November, which had previously seen the continuation of Samhain festivities begun the night before and which formed the majority of the sabbat, and renamed it All Saints' Day. Later on, they would claim the entirety of Samhain for the church (Kiger,

2020), expanding their rebrand to the night of October 31, and calling it All Hallows Day Evening, a name which would eventually be shortened to All Hallows' Eve (even further down the line, this would evolve into the Halloween we know today, but more on that later).

It is important to note that while the transition from the Pagan Samhain to the Catholic All Saints' Day may sound as though it happened without any real hiccups, the truth is that there were many bumps, scrapes, and misfortunes along the way. The first of these pertains to the Druids of Ancient Celtic culture. Think back to Chapter Two, where we learned that, given all the duties they performed and functions they fulfilled, the Druids could be regarded as inhabiting the same space in Celtic culture that priests do in the structure of the Roman Catholic Church. After the advent of Christianity in Ireland, however, the Druids were treated with a large degree of mistrust. This was because they were regarded as the group most likely to persevere with the observance of the ancient Druidic and Pagan beliefs, practices, and holidays. Fortunately, the Druids moved proactively, and in order to quell the fears of the church, a large number of them converted to Christianity and joined the monastic order, changing from Druids to monks (De Souza Soares, 2013). While it is unfortunate that they were forced to abandon their traditions and beliefs almost entirely, it was because of their conversion that we even know about Druids today. Before, the Druidic religion was passed on by means of oral tradition. Once they began studying under the tutelage of the Catholic priests, they were able to put pen to paper and create records of their history. These records have endured and formed the basis of the knowledge we possess of Druidry and Paganism today.

The church changed more than just the name of the festival, altering the meaning of many of the rituals and traditions performed during the sabbat. Most prominently, while the festival retained its connection to the Otherworld, as well as the belief that supernatural entities crossed over into our world, they were now said to be evil, and that festivities should include Christian practices aimed at warding them off and keeping observers safe from their malevolent influence (Clan Campbell Society, n.d.). In contrast to this gentler change made by the church, a blanket ban was placed on all divinatory practices, not only on Samhain, but throughout the entire year. As we know, divination was a time-honored Druidic tradition, as they used these rituals in order to suss out the provenance they needed to undertake for the year that lay ahead. Sadly, the Catholic church essentially outlawed divination, as they believed that all methods of fortune telling were demonic in nature, and that communing with the dead in this manner was nothing but dangerous. It was also said if divination did indeed reveal the future, the only things which would be shown were falsehoods (De Souza Soares, 2013).

As time wore on, more and more of the Ancient Celtic religious constructs were subsumed into the Catholic dogma. Continuous changes were made to the beliefs surrounding Samhain. For instance, given the importance of the Otherworld in the festivities of the sabbat, the Catholics consolidated Pagan views of the afterlife with their own, eventually replacing it with the Christian concept of Hell. However, despite their best efforts, Christian missionaries and officials were unable to eradicate Samhain entirely. They understood that, while many Ancient Celts had converted to Christianity, many of them still believed in the teachings of Paganism. There was a solid foundation for this, as Paganism is by nature a polytheistic religion. As such, many former Pagans simply included the worship of the Christian God alongside that of their own deities. Fearing their efforts to remake Samhain into a different festival, as well as this continued silent polytheistic devotion, the Catholic church claimed the day after Samhain as well, turning the second day of November into All Souls Day. Cleverly, they incorporated aspects of Samhain festivities into this new holy day. All Souls Day was denoted as the day when the living were meant to pray for and celebrate the souls of the departed. Essentially, the ancestral veneration practiced by Pagans and Druids during Samhain was moved to this day and recontextualized to align with the Catholic teachings of the afterlife, including the Christian Heaven and Hell. Similarly, the church took hold of the Pagan midsummer festival, renaming it Saint John's Day (Clan Campbell Society, n.d.).

These changes implemented by the Catholic church paved the way for Samhain to evolve and change even more. As the centuries passed by, the original tenets of the festival became increasingly obscured until modern incarnations of the sabbat have become largely independent from the ancient Pagan and Druidic seasonal harvest festival. In fact, one of the most famous parables related to Irish Catholicism is a metaphor for the wide-ranging cultural and religious renovations implemented after their arrival on the island. In the parable, Saint Patrick (otherwise known as the patron saint of Ireland) is said to have all the snakes out of Ireland after he arrived to spread the gospel of the church. While a literal interpretation may very well be possible, many believe that the snakes are said to be symbolic (De Souza Soares, 2013) of the native Pagan and Druidic religions that were present in Ireland in the pre-Christian era. Though we know now that these religions were not entirely eradicated, and that they managed to survive the test of time, the sheer fame of the parable effectively demonstrates just how strongly the Catholic church succeeded in their mission of conversion and construction.

Modern Christians and the Festival of Samhain

The Catholic reformation of Samhain had extremely long-lasting effects, to the extent that the version of Samhain celebrated today, more popularly known as Halloween, relies almost entirely on the practices established by the missionaries all those centuries ago.

Modern-day Halloween has its roots in the culture of a post-Christianized Ireland. For centuries, holidays such as All Hallows' Eve, All Saints' Day, and All Souls' Day were celebrated in the place of the traditional Samhain. In fact, the name 'Halloween' is derived from that of All Hallows' Eve, and is a contraction of the longer name which has come to be considered outdated. Nowadays, Halloween is used not only because of its simpler nature, but also because it is more indicative of the secular nature of the holiday. All Hallows' Eve connects the day to its older Catholic form, while Halloween separates the festivities from the church and ties it more closely to the candy-infused celebration we know today.

Now that we understand how Halloween came into its name, we can examine how exactly the last day of October evolved into, well, Halloween. Regrettably, the fun-filled festival we know and love today was catalyzed by one of the worst events in Irish history: the potato famine. With crops dying on a mass scale, the quality of living in Ireland fell sharply. Out of desperation, large swathes of the population left their homeland in search of better, more nourishing shores. In this mass exodus, many Irish people crossed the ocean and settled in the United States. These immigrants brought with them the ways of celebrating the festival of All Hallows' Eve as they had been taught back in Catholic Ireland. When they arrived on the American shores, the inhabitants of the New World were strangers to all Celtic festivals, especially those rooted in Pagan and Druidic tradition. Over time, as the Irish-

American community grew and became more firmly rooted in the American cultural landscape, their customs and beliefs permeated the consciousness of society, and Samhain traveled into that consciousness along with the rest (De Souza Soares, 2013).

Eventually, All Hallows' Eve found its place in the American social calendar. Initially, the holy holiday was celebrated only in its original (in a manner of speaking) Catholic capacity. As knowledge of the holiday grew, the celebrations of All Hallows' Eve, and by extension Samhain, were adapted once again. This time, they were made to suit the sensibilities of the American public. As the celebrations were modernized, they were also secularized, and in the 1930s, the modern Halloween was born. That being said, the holiday we know today only took on its shape in 1950 (De Souza Soares, 2013), when it was adapted on a grand scale once more, this time to appeal to the youth, a demographic to whom Halloween is still one of the high points of the year. With this move towards younger people, the festival increased in its secularity, with the conservative values of the society of the day encouraging the elimination of those elements of Halloween which may be considered too overwhelming or fear-inducing for children.

A number of Irish traditions were adopted by and adapted for American Halloween. Today, the first of these traditions, none other than the Jack O' Lantern, may be regarded as the symbol of Halloween. In America, pumpkins are carved, as they align more closely with the other vegetables represented in the harvest cornucopias often seen at this time of the year. Here the celebration of the harvest is more popularly linked to Thanksgiving, but given the original spirit in which Samhain was celebrated, harvest pumpkins work for Halloween as well. In the Ancient Celtic tradition, potatoes or turnips were carved. In both instances, candles are placed inside and lit, the fire representing the positive, nourishing powers of the sun (Kiger, 2020). By placing the candle inside the carved vegetable, you are essentially imbuing the harvest with this holy power. Additionally, these vegetable lanterns were also intended to ward off a spirit known as Stingy Jack, who was refused entry to both Heaven and Hell, and consequently wanders the Earth. To most Americans, Jack O' Lanterns are simply pieces of decoration, representing only their commitment to the Halloween festivities.

Another Halloween tradition, that of trick-or-treating, was also taken across the waters by the Irish-Catholic immigrants. Originally, in this Celtic tradition, food was provided for the spirits, creatures, and deities which wandered the Earth on Samhain (think something along the lines of a more informal dumb supper), but as the festival took on a more secular tone, these appeasing morsels were swapped out in favor of candy.

Finally, we take a look at the most well-known tradition of Halloween: costumes. Though post-Christian celebrations of Samhain warned people that the supernatural creatures who roamed around that night were malevolent, people eventually began to leave their house during the festival, wearing costumes that represented the very things they were meant to fear. They would go door-to-door, jokingly asking for the food which was meant to appease them (De Souza Soares, 2013). Once again, as the holiday departed from its religious roots, the practice of dressing up as those creatures thought to be roaming the Earth lost its potency. While many do still don apparel meant to represent witches, fairies, and ghosts, they enter the world alongside superheroes, characters from film and television, as well as figures from popular culture. Now, these costumes are worn for nothing more than fun, and mean nothing more than a treat-filled night on the town.

Halloween is best-known today for the collection of candy and the binge-watching of slasher films. While this type of celebration is the one that appeals to the majority of people, there are still a large number who are devoted to the older, more traditional Catholic celebration. By now, if there is one thing that should be evident about Samhain, it is that the festival, regardless of incarnation, is malleable. There is a certain art to celebrating the sabbat, and art is nothing if not subjective.

Key Takeaways

- When Christian missionaries arrived in Ireland with the purpose of evangelizing, they found that they had to change tack in order to succeed. To that end, they decided to adopt established Pagan and Druidic practices and Christianize them.

- Samhain underwent a large number of changes, with October 31st becoming All Hallows' Eve, November 1st becoming All Saints' Day, and November 2nd becoming All Souls' Day.

- Rituals practiced at Samhain were also Christianized, with the Druidic veneration of the dead and the belief in creatures crossing over into our world described as evil.

- Due to the Irish Potato Famine, a large number of Irish-Catholics fled to the United States. There, they continued their post-Christian celebrations of Samhain.

- Over time, the Catholic version of Samhain came to be known as Halloween.

- The further Halloween entered into the American cultural vernacular, the further it diverted from its religious roots. Soon, it became the secular festival that is celebrated today.

- Some of the Samhain traditions that were secularized and Americanized were that of Jack O' Lanterns, trick-or-treating, and the wearing of costumes representing things other than supernatural creatures or spirits, such as superheroes or figures in popular culture.

- While there are still many Catholic people who observe All Hallows' Eve and other, post-Christian versions of Samhain, Halloween is the more popular, more mainstream festival.

CHAPTER 4:

Samhain Around the World

Those we love never truly leave us. There are things that death cannot touch. —Jack Thorne

In the previous chapter, we learned how Samhain spread to another part of the world through the immigration of Irish Catholics to the United States. While their arrival there helped the already modified All Hallows' Eve evolve into the modern-day Halloween, festivals like Samhain have existed across the globe for millennia. Today, Samhain and Halloween are celebrated all over the world, largely due to the increase in globalization that has occurred in the last century. However, before the sabbat was able to spread this far, other festivals like it were already being observed in a variety of cultures. In this chapter, we will explore the different cultural and religious festivals that resemble Samhain. We will focus on the celebration of the Day of the Dead by indigenous Latin cultures, as well as ancestral holidays observed in Europe, Africa, and Asia.

The World and Samhain

Before we begin this exploration, it is important to understand that while Samhain is now an international festival, there are still many cultures that have a festival just like it, and that choose to practice their traditional rituals instead. That being said, you will find many similarities between these customs and that of Samhain. If nothing else, this shows us how celebrations of the departed and the veneration of ancestors transcend cultural and religious barriers. Though no two festivals will be exactly the same, the foundational beliefs underlying each of them are nonetheless connected.

Indigenous Celebrations

The first stop on our world tour of Samhain-adjacent festivals takes us to Latin America, more specifically, Mexico. After Samhain, the Mexican ancestral holiday is perhaps the most well-known internationally. Commonly known as Día de los Muertos, the Latin holiday has roots that stretch back centuries.

Día de los Muertos finds its origins in Mesoamerican rituals, but over time evolved to include European religious practices, as well as aspects of Spanish culture. Celebrations of the holiday can be traced back approximately 3,000 years, beginning with the people of Mesoamerican in the pre-Columbian age and their interpretations of death and its nature. According to the traditional beliefs held by the Aztec and Nahua peoples, time and the universe are both cyclical in nature, with death forming part of this cosmic circle (History.com Editors, 2018b). Given this view, the indigenous peoples of Mexico held the belief that death was ever-present and important to the normal, healthy functioning of human life. Indigenous beliefs regarded death as a journey, essentially a continuation of the journey that makes up the mortal lifespan. The journey of death sent the departed soul to Chicunamictlán, the land of the dead. If you want to connect Día de los Muertos to Samhain, think of the realm as equivalent to the Pagan and Druidic Otherworld. Upon their arrival in the land of the dead, souls were tasked with undergoing another journey, one in which they had to pass through nine different levels. This posthumous odyssey is said to have the potential to last several years, and souls must make it all the way through those nine levels before they are able to arrive at Mictlán (History.com Editors, 2018b), the realm of everlasting rest.

Centuries later, the Spanish conquistadors arrived in Mexico, and brought with them their own traditions and rituals used to honor and celebrate their dead. These European colonizers were Catholic, and brought with them that particular religious interpretation of the afterlife. One of their contributions to the festival of Día de los Muertos was the food they prepared as a means of honoring the dead. In Spain, the practice is to bake something known as 'spirit bread' (*pan de ánimas*), which they would then bring to cemeteries and place on the graves of their loved ones on All Souls' Day (History.com Editors, 2018b). In addition to this, graves would be decorated with flowers and lit candles, lighting the path the souls of the dead would travel as they made their way to Earth on the holy day. To this very day, flowers and candlelight play an integral role in celebrations of Día de los Muertos. As we saw in Chapter 3, the church held a darker view of the afterlife, dividing it into the concepts of heaven and hell, which we can see stands in stark contrast to the view held by indigenous Mexicans. As time passed, the indigenous celebrations underwent the same types of changes implemented by Catholic missionaries in Ireland. However, there is an important distinction between the evolution of Día de los Muertos and that of Samhain. Where in Ireland, Samhain was seemingly supplanted by the Catholic ancestral festival, Día de los Muertos emerged in Mexico as a hybrid festival, containing components of practice from each contributing culture.

The first marker of this mixed nature is the date on which Día de los Muertos begins: October 31st. In Mexican practice, it is believed that the gates of heaven open at midnight on the last night of October, aligning with the Catholic celebration (Ventures, 2019) of All Hallows' Eve. The festival then extends to November 2nd, and festivities end alongside those observed on All Souls' Day. Given the fact that Día de los Muertos is a celebratory entity that exists semi-independently from the Catholic holy days, the days of the festival have different designations, each related more closely to the original, indigenous incarnation. Firstly, celebrations begin as the last day of October draws to a close. At the stroke of midnight, when the month changes, Día de los Angelitos (the day of the little angels) is observed. On this day, it is said that the souls of deceased children may enter the world through the opened gates of heaven. In these 24 hours, these young souls are reunited with their families, who celebrate the time they had together. When the day of the little angels comes to an end, Día de los Difuntos begins. On November 2nd, the day of the deceased begins, and adult souls visit the homes of their loved ones. Similar to the children's day, the visiting souls are celebrated by those they have left behind. At noon the same day, the festival enters its final designated stage, the eponymous Día de los Muertos, during which the souls of all the dead are acknowledged and venerated (Ventures, 2019).

The festivities of Día de los Muertos are centered around the celebration of these souls, each on their own day. Connected to these festivities are specific rituals which may be undertaken in order to celebrate the dead. Ranging from preparing and eating different types of food to building altars of remembrance, each and every ritual performed is made up of an array of different elements, each with their own spiritual or cultural significance.

We begin with the construction of altars that celebrate the dead, which forms the most important and potent ritual in the entire festival. Commonly known as *ofrendas*, which translates to offerings, creating these altars is a group activity usually undertaken by families. The purpose of the ofrenda is that of encouragement, with families hoping to entice their deceased loved ones back from the afterlife so that the prayers of the family may be heard, and the ones they lost may return, partake of the sacramental food and participate in the festivities honoring them, and all those who have crossed over.

Altars are adorned with a variety of decorations, the most universal of which is the Mexican marigold. Colloquially referred to as *la flor de muerto*, the marigold is said to act as a floral beacon, with its bright colors and rich scent attracting the souls of the deceased. Marigolds are effectively guiding light, helping usher souls towards the altars where their favorite foods have been laid out, ready to be feasted on by the departed. There is some symbolism attached to the use of marigolds as well (Ventures, 2019), as they are believed to represent the beautiful and fragile nature of human life. Marigolds are indigenous to Mexico, making their importance to Día de los Muertos celebrations a clear and distinct indication of how deeply connected the custom is to the land and its people.

When the altars are built, usually on October 30th or 31st, families begin by covering a table with an oilcloth, ordinarily one that contains one or several bright colors. On top of this oilcloth, the components of the altar are placed, with each one representing something that was dear to or important about the person being celebrated. Items used for the altar include photographs of the deceased, as well as some of their personal belongings. These items are not simply placed randomly on the tabletop. Instead, the altar is divided into two, with the upper section being used to place the aforementioned items, and the lower section being filled with traditional Mexican offerings. These offerings may include traditional Mexican food items, *calaveras* (skulls) and other items which reflect the personality, sensibility, and interests of the person to whom the altar is dedicated.

The skull is an important symbol in the lore of the Day of the Dead. In addition to those fashioned out of clay, which are primarily used in altars, skulls are also crafted from sugar and eaten as candy or included in altars as part of the ofrendas. Skulls are also very often used as motifs for face painting. Observers will paint their faces to look like skulls and will wear this face paint (Ventures, 2019) when attending the lively, colorful parades and parties that characterize celebrations of the Mexican festival. While calaveras have historically formed part of the festivities, the design most frequently used today was actually created in 1910 by printer and cartoonist José Guadalupe Posada, who utilized the skull in his work as a means of political commentary. Eventually, his creation, known as 'La Calavera Catrina,' was adopted by festival goers, and the design has been a staple of Día de los Muertos ever since (History.com

Editors, 2018b). In addition to the skull, a popular symbol used during the holiday is also that of the skeleton, known in Spanish as the *calaca*.

Other symbols used during festivities include the following:

- Crops are used to represent the Earth, and their scents are believed to nourish the visiting souls. Seeds are often placed on altars to feed birds.

- Moving objects are placed on altars to represent the air or the wind. A popular object used is tissue paper (*papel picado* in Spanish), which is cut into different shapes and traditional icons, such as butterflies.

- Water is often placed on altars to be used as hydration for souls, who are said to be thirsty after their travels to the world of the living.

- Wax candles are placed on altars, their flames completing the presence of the elements. A candle is lit for each soul being remembered during the festival, with an extra candle being included for those souls that have been forgotten.

- Butterflies are also represented in many altars and decorations, as souls are thought to return in this form when they visit their altars and loved ones.

If there are two things that we must take away from all this is that Día de los Muertos is a vibrant and beautiful festival that seeks to take away some of the heaviness and depression that accompanies the death of someone we love. The second thing we must realize is that while indigenous Mexican celebrations of death, as well as Samhain were influenced in the same ways by the Catholic church, the festivals that evolved from this influence, namely Día de los Muertos and Halloween, are different festivals, each with their own rites, rituals and cultural significance.

Samhain in Europe

On the European continent, as well as the island of the United Kingdom, Samhain is still celebrated, more or less in the same way it was by the Ancient Celtic people. In those places where this traditional Samhain is not observed, people celebrate the Catholic holidays or Halloween. Given the fact that Samhain originated in Europe with the Ancient Celts, whose population spread from Ireland through France, Portugal, and Italy all the way to Eastern Europe, it is expected that it would be the most common ancestral festival on the continent. That being said, Samhain is not universally observed, as we already know. The festival that resembles it most closely, and that serves our purposes in this book the best, is that of the Blessed Easte–also known as the Easter of the Blessed Ones–that is celebrated in Moldova and Bukovina (a historical region that today covers parts of Romania and the Ukraine).

Known in Eastern Europe as *Paștele blajinilor*, the Blessed Easter is celebrated on the Monday following Saint Thomas Sunday, placing the festival roughly eight days after the Orthodox Church has observed and celebrated their own Easter. It is important to note that while the Blessed Easter has religious underpinnings, with celebrations taking place in church graveyards, the holiday exists independently of any particular religious body (Blessed Easter *(Pashtele Blajinilor)*, 2023). We can, however, see some resemblance between this festival and that of Samhain. Where Samhain was used by the Ancient Celtic people to bid farewell to the 'light part' of the year, and to mark the beginning of the 'dark part,' so is the Blessed Easter also divided into sections of light and dark. All festivities take place in the 'dark week,' also known as *săptămâna neagră*. This week is preceded by the 'light week', or *săptămâna luminată*, during which people are meant to abstain from any and all work on the domestic as well as agricultural fronts. Think of it as a sort of fasting for a non-religious Lent. While taking a week's worth of rest is intended to act in part as a means of spiritual cleansing, it is also believed that if work is undertaken during the light week, a person might run the risk of going blind. This blindness is thought to be brought on by the deceased who have been disrespected by the work, which interferes with the time of remembrance during the light week (Global Informality Project, 2022).

While the Easter of the Blessed Ones is a centuries-old tradition, today it has largely been disregarded by younger generations, and the majority of observers come from older, more tradition-oriented generations (Global Informality Project, 2022). That being said, celebrants both old and young adhere to the same time-honored rituals when observing the holiday. The first of these rituals involves putting together parcels called *pomeni*, which will be taken to the cemeteries when the celebrations begin (Global Informality Project, 2022). The pomeni, the name of which is Slavic in origin and which translates to 'handouts,' are made up hard-boiled, painted eggs; breads that have been braided into a round (known locally as *colaci*); a small towel, usually made of cotton; some pieces of candy and a candle with some matches. The entire package is usually wrapped in a plastic bag. Traditionally, the pomeni contain these basic elements, though they may be personalized to better honor the deceased. In modern celebrations, many people have opted to include more expensive, high-ticket items such as electronic devices and other expensive gifts. In some instances, these items have replaced the traditional pomeni elements. It is unclear if these displays of wealth are meant to impress the living or the dead, but they are included nonetheless. According to Moldovan and Romanian customs, the pomeni are handed to other visitors in the cemetery when visiting the graves of deceased loved ones. When the parcel is handed over, the giver accompanies the gesture with the words *pentru sufletul* or *For the soul of*, which they then follow with the name of the deceased person who is being honored. The person receiving the pomeni responds with the phrase *bodaproste*, a shortened Russian phrase that translates to 'may God forgive.'

In addition to the making and exchanging of pomeni, the celebrations for the Blessed Easter include performing maintenance on the gravesites of deceased family members. The graves and tombstones are spruced up, with old flowers being replaced, weeds being removed from the grass, and the headstone being given a touch-up (Global Informality Project, 2022). Relatives of the deceased also often light a candle near the grave, and food and wine are also brought to the cemetery. The wine is poured out over the grave and tombstone, as it is believed that the devil will consume the wine and become too intoxicated to claim the living souls of the deceased's relatives. Some people believe that the wine is actually consumed by the departed souls, allowing them to join in the celebrations.

Whenever food is brought to cemeteries during the Blessed Easter, the goal is for the living and the dead to share a meal. In order to do this, the ancestors must be called to their place of earthly rest. Calling the ancestors involves dying eggshells red and releasing them into the river, allowing them to float downstream. While this is the most popular method (and certainly the one with the most showmanship), other people call upon their forebears by placing their ears against the ground in order to hear the movement of the souls. The reason why this practice is used less often is that the sound of the spirits' voices is said to be capable of making the living deaf (Global Informality Project, 2022). While this belief must not be scoffed at or disregarded, it is possible that the eggshell method is preferred because it requires significantly more effort. Effort is of the utmost importance to celebrations of the Blessed Easter, as the less effort that is put in, the more likely it will be that in the year that follows, crops and livestock will suffer and die, and the hands and feet of those people who shirked their ancestral responsibilities will become riddled with aching pains.

The Easter of the Blessed Ones remains a vital celebration in the traditional Eastern European calendar, despite its dwindling popularity. Although it differs from Samhain in many ways, the core tenets of the two festivals align very closely, and when all the differences and divergences are stripped away, the same thing emerges as the most important: the veneration and celebration of what came before.

Samhain in Africa

Festivals resembling Samhain have been around for an extremely long time, and may be dated back millenia. In this section, we will explore some of the historic festivals as they are celebrated in Africa. In particular, we will examine the Adae and Wag festivals.

Akwasidae and Awukudae

The Akan and Ashanti cultures of West Africa celebrate the Adae festival, whose name translates to 'resting place' in English. This festival, which is subdivided into the holidays of Akwasidae and Awukudae (Amgborale Blay, 2014), is centered around the ancestral spirits and involves invoking and celebrating them. Within the calendar of the Akan people, one year consists of nine different cycles, with each cycle lasting approximately 42 days. Adae festivals are celebrated twice during each respective cycle, with Akwasidae being observed on a Sunday, and Awukudae observed on a Wednesday.

On the day of the celebration, traditional leaders enter the place of the ancestors' rest, bringing them offerings of food and drink intended to represent the reverence of their people. While the leaders are invoking and honoring the spirits, the remainders of the community utilize the day as one of rest, as all work is forbidden on the days of Adae. These celebrations, and each of the others that are traditionally undertaken during the festival, are carried out within distinct communities. When Akwasidae and Awukudae are being celebrated, there is no grand display that brings together different peoples. Rather, the traditional leaders perform their duties within the confines of their own communities. Similar to Samhain, on the days when the Adae festivals are celebrated, conflicts of all kinds are discouraged. Where truly unignorable instances of conflict exist, an opportunity is granted for all those involved in the dispute to gather before the traditional leaders and the community (Amgborale Blay, 2014) in order to work through the issues. Though the two smaller festivals are observed in a regional capacity, the Akan year culminates with a larger, integrated festival: Adae Kese. We will return to this festival in a moment.

When looking at Akwasidae and Awukudae, we can see that the former is slightly larger than the latter, given the fact that much of its celebrations take place in public spaces. Though these communal festivities are what the majority of people look forward to the most, the rituals that are actually most integral to the Adae festivals are performed in private, in the burial place of the ancestors. On festival days, traditional leaders enter these places and, in addition to performing (Amgborale Blay, 2014) the nourishment ritual, bare their shoulders and remove their sandals to indicate their respect for the deceased. The ancestral spirits are invoked by the leader, who calls upon each of them in turn and offers them a drink. A ritualistic offering is made, with the remnants thereof being placed on the stools inside the resting place, along with dishes which have been prepared in honor of the spirits. Once the ritual has been completed, the leader takes up a seated position, as if he is sitting in state, so that he may more easily receive the ancestral spirits who will be arriving in visitation.

Preparations for the festival are a community effort and often involve the playing of ritual drums that announce the impending festivities and invoke the spirits of ancestral drummers, asking for their blessings. The public celebrations included in Adae festivals involve a large quantity of singing, dancing, and playing music. After the somber traditions have been observed in the ancestral resting place, lively festivities take place in order to unite the communities of the living and the dead. Though these celebrations often feel very light-hearted, they perform an important function by keeping the community connected to the spirits of their ancestors.

At the end of the Akan year, Adac Kcse is celebrated. The festival, whose name means 'Great Adae' in English, performs a function similar to Samhain in that it marks the end of the nine cycles comprising the Akan year (Amgboralc Blay, 2014). In this time, public celebrations and lively parades are held again, but the festival also marks a time for a quieter, more private introspection. Celebrators are encouraged to look inwards and take stock of the year that has passed.

Wag and Wafaa Al Nil

The Egyptian festival of the Wag dates back to ancient times, and honors the death of god Osiris. Originally celebrated during the age of the Old Kingdom between the years of 2572 and 2130 BC, Ancient Egyptians celebrated Wag during Thout, the first month of the year according to the Coptic calendar. Although the festival commonly occurred during this time, its celebration was actually dependent (History of Egypt, n.d.) on the water levels of the Nile River, as many of the festivities made use of this body of water.

The festival of the Wag resembles Samhain in that both festivals provide people with the opportunity to honor the dead as they make their way to the afterlife. Celebrations of the festival are also centered around Osiris, the god of Fertility, Agriculture, and the Dead. Osiris was married to the goddess Isis, who scoured the corners of Egypt for the parts of Osiris' body after his death. Egyptian lore holds that the flooding of the Nile, which influences the time when the festival is held, is brought on by the tears of mourning shed by Isis. In addition to this, the Egyptian belief of reincarnation stems from the goddess' successful efforts to bring her husband back to life.

Today, the festival mainly exists in two different forms. The first, also called Wag, is celebrated by a group known as Kemetic Reconstructionists. Members of this group, which is a subdivision of Neo-Paganism (*WAG: Egyptian Festival of the Dead*, 2022), adhere to the same basic religious tenets as those observed by the population of Ancient Egypt, using modern translations of ancient texts to guide their beliefs and rituals. Interestingly, some Kemetic Reconstructionists have taken elements of Ancient Egyptian religion and arranged them according to the Wiccan structure of worship. In this instance, practitioners follow the calendrical format of the Wheel of the Year, but have turned their veneration towards Egyptian deities. Modern celebrations of Wag involve the hosting of a feast; floating a paper boat down a river in tribute to Isis and Osiris, and visiting cemeteries and the gravesites of deceased loved ones and ancestors. The second modern interpretation of Wag presents itself in the form of Wafaa Al Nil, meaning Fidelity of the Nile. This festival is celebrated by contemporary Egyptians during the month of August, and celebrates the flooding of the Nile River. Wafaa Al Nil festivities (*WAG: Egyptian Festival of the Dead*, 2022) involve music and dancing, with attendees often dressed in traditional Egyptian garb. During August of every year, the festival attracts a large number of people from all over the world. In addition to the lively festivals held in honor of Wafaa Al Nil, modern celebrations include a tradition taken directly from the ancient incarnation of Wag. In this practice, small paper boats are made. These boats are then either placed on the western side of gravesites in honor of Osiris' death or floated down the waters of the Nile for the same purposes of veneration. Celebrators come to Egypt to participate in these festivities and to honor the Ancient Egyptian gods at the holy site that is the Nile River.

Samhain in Asia

Throughout Asia, there are a number of traditional festivals that perform the same ritualistic function as Samhain. In this section, we will explore the festivals of Obon, Chuseok, and the Hungry Ghost Festival (Geiling, 2014).

Obon

The Obon Festival is a traditional Buddhist celebration that is observed in Japan, being sometimes referred to as the Japanese Day of the Dead. The festival is celebrated during the seventh month of the lunar calendar, which equates to August on the Gregorian calendar. Traditionally celebrated on the 15th day of the month, Obon festivities often begin on the 13th of August and may last up until August 16 (Geiling, 2014). During the time of the festival, it is said that the spirits of the ancestors return to Earth to visit their living family members, who remember and honor them in observance of the festival. The familial structure is essential to celebrating Obon properly, and as such, many people choose to return to their childhood homes and hometowns for the duration of the festival. In a ritual that bears a striking resemblance to one of those practiced during Samhain, large bonfires are lit as a part of Obon festivities. According to traditional Japanese Buddhist beliefs, the element of fire acts as a guide, helping to lead the ancestral spirits back to the earthly realm. Also similar to Samhain, Obon includes public celebrations, an important component of which is the *bon-odor*, a traditional Japanese dance that welcomes the visiting spirits. Lanterns, known as *toro nagashi*, are also constructed and then sent down rivers toward the ocean.

Chuseok

Celebrated in both North and South Korea, Chuseok is another Asian ancestral festival. The festival takes place in the eighth lunar month, ordinarily on the 15th day. According to the Gregorian calendar, this places Chuseok in the middle of September or October. Ancestors are venerated through means of food, song, and dance, the latter two of which often take place in public parades consisting of people dressed in traditional Korean garb

(Geiling, 2014). We highlight this festival because it resembles Samhain, and while the ancestral aspect is certainly something the two have in common, Chuseok also resembles the Ancient Celtic festival in that the harvest is celebrated at this time. Over the course of three days, participants in Chuseok give thanks to their ancestors for the harvest, as it is believed that their spiritual forces aid in the cultivation and delivering of healthy crops. Harvest celebrations are held communally, with different families coming together to share a meal in honor of their forebears. Throughout the days of Chuseok, people visit the graves of family members, cleaning the gravesites and paying tribute to those who came before them. Once the sun sets, the revelry begins, and folk games are played and traditional dances are performed.

The Hungry Ghost Festival

The final Samhain-esque festival we will examine stands out among all the rest we've explored due simply to its length. In the Buddhist and Taoist religions, an entire calendar month is devoted to the observance of an ancestral festival (Geiling, 2014). Hungry Ghost Month covers the sixth lunar month, and its culminating celebration, the Hungry Ghost Festival, falls on the 15th day. Translated to modern calendrical measures, this means that the festival is usually celebrated in either July or August in China.

While the entire Hungry Ghost Month is dedicated to ancestral reverence, it all builds up to the final festival, when the gates between the netherworld and the mortal world are opened at their greatest. On the night of the Hungry Ghost Festival, while the majority of people are engaged in celebration, a number of others remain inside their homes, fearful that they will be found and haunted by spirits who have slipped through the gates.

Despite this darker outlook that some people may have, the Hungry Ghost Festival is an overall jovial occurrence. Festivities are kicked off by a parade, followed by lanterns being placed onto floats and sent out onto the water. The lanterns form an important part of the festival, as each family observes their individual lantern, believing that the longer the lantern takes to catch on fire entirely, the more prosperity lies in store for them in the year to come.

Like Samhain, food plays an important part in the Hungry Ghost Festival. Families construct altars on which they place food in order to ask for goodwill from the ancestral spirits. In addition to this, paper items such as false money, paper cars and watches are placed into metal drums, and the items are set aflame. This burning is a sort of ritual sacrifice, with the items being offered up as gifts for the ancestors.

From our travels through the world in this chapter, we can see that the celebration of festivals like Samhain is not limited to the Ancient Celtic people, or indeed their descendants. All over the world, people make time to honor their ancestors, reflect on the time that has passed, and turn their eyes, hearts, and hopes to the times that lie ahead.

Key Takeaways

- Festivals like Samhain are not unique to Ancient Celtic culture, as different iterations of this type of ancestral and seasonal harvest festival can be found all over the world.

- In Latin America, Día de los Muertos is celebrated, finding its origins in indigenous customs and beliefs which were mixed with those of Spanish Catholic missionaries. El Día de los Muertos is the festival that most closely resembles Samhain.

- In Europe, Samhain is still celebrated in many countries. In certain parts of Eastern Europe, however, the Easter of the Blessed Ones is celebrated. This festival is celebrated mainly in Moldova, Romania, and the Ukraine, and is centered around communing with and celebrating deceased family members.

- In Africa, we find the festivals of Akwasidae, Awukudae, Wag, and Wafaa Al Nil. Both festivals have been around for centuries, with the former two being celebrated in Western Africa, and the latter two in Northern Africa. All four festivals are rooted in traditional practices, but have evolved over time to include modern rites and rituals as well.

- In Asia, the Samhain-esque festivals of Obon, Chuseok, and the Hungry Ghost Festival are celebrated. Each of these festivals involve celebration on a public, as well as private, family level. These festivals aim to invoke ancestral spirits and thank them for their contributions to the prosperity of their living descendants.

- Though each of these holidays and festivals have their own distinctive and unique beliefs and practices, they all contain the same fundamental perspective: ancestral veneration.

CHAPTER 5:

Samhain Structures – Natural Materials

In the spring and summer, the focus might be on abundance and fiery action, but at Samhain, we begin to turn inward and become more reflective. –Tenae Stewart

The festival of Samhain is inextricably linked to nature. Though festivities might focus more on the metaphysical realms of death and time, celebrations are rooted in the powers of the natural world (Evert Hopman, 2021). This chapter will explore the different flowers, herbs, crystals, and other plants that are tied to Samhain. We will examine the use of each natural material and the ways in which it may be integrated into celebrations of the festival, whether individual or communal.

Sourcing Samhain

When preparing for your Samhain festivities, you will be looking for the different components and ingredients that will enable you to experience the festival at its full potency. In your preparation, you need look no further for these items than the kingdom of Mother Nature. From the store that is the great outdoors, you will find everything you need to celebrate Samhain the way it was intended. Because Samhain is celebrated in the fall, many of its natural materials will be either seasonal or of such a nature that it reflects the darker, colder time of the year that begins with the sabbat.

Samhain Herbs

Herbs can be used for Samhain in a myriad of ways. While the majority of their uses are ritualistic, if you'd like, some herbs can be incorporated into the food prepared for Samhain feasts and dumb suppers. Remember that rites and rituals are flexible, and that you are free to pick and choose which of the herbs listed below you want to use when preparing for and celebrating Samhain.

Rosemary

The rosemary herb is often used in holistic and esoteric ritual practice for the purposes of smudging (Wigington, 2019). While it does have powerful protective properties, rosemary may also be used during Samhain as it holds a strong connection to the act of remembrance.

When preparing for Samhain, bind bundles of rosemary together and place them on your ancestral altar. Its presence there will strengthen the connection you will feel to your ancestral spirits who visit when the veil between worlds thins. Alternatively, use rosemary as a supplement in incense mixtures. Burning this incense during the sabbat will perform the same function as the bundles placed on the altar.

The herb also has potent healing properties. In the time leading up to the new year, construct medicinal healing poppets using rosemary. If you are celebrating Samhain with friends or family, make this into a group activity in order to foster a greater sense of unity and connection.

Mugwort

Known by a number of names, including felon herb, wild wormwood, cronewort, and Saint John's Plant, mugwort is a powerful divinatory tool (Wigington, 2019). Mugwort possesses the power to alter our dreams in order to bring us closer to the supernatural realm. Given how thin the interwordly veil is at the time of Samhain, this herb may help you to come in closer contact with spirits and entities from across the metaphysical way.

Mugwort is most commonly used in teas, and if you're up for some supernaturally-influenced slumber, drink a cup of tea containing the herb before you go to sleep. It is important that you do not just drink the tea and hope for the best. Because spirits of all inclinations abound during the sabbat, it is imperative that you set some intentions when drinking mugwort tea. This will help to guide your dream experiences and steer you away from those entities that would wish to do you harm. Alternatively, you could blend mugwort into a mix of essential oils for use during a massage. If you choose this route, your best bet would be to take dried mugwort and incorporate it into some olive oil. Mugwort can also be used in aromatherapy, and you can usually find aromatic mugwort wands for sale if you don't feel up to making your own. If you would like to take the tea approach and give it a human spin, before bed, draw yourself a warm bath and infuse the water with the herb. Regardless of your preferred method of use, mugwort is sure to provide you with some amazing metaphysical encounters.

Star Anise

Also known as Chinese Star Anise, this spice is obtained from the fruit of an evergreen tree endemic to China, and makes its appearance in the food prepared to celebrate Samhain and its Mexican sister-festival Día de los Muertos (Evert Hopman, 2021).

Known as Pan de Muerto, or Bread of the Dead, Star Anise is incorporated into the recipe for its spiritual significance. The spice has been in use for centuries, and has a wide variety of functions from providing spiritual protection to enhancing a person's psychic energy and ability for spiritual connection and communication. Star Anise is also said to be able to bring its users good luck. All of these attributes align with the purposes of Samhain festivals. By preparing bread or other foods using Star Anise, these effects may be gifted to all those who consume the dishes. Additionally, the spice is often powdered and infused into incense mixtures. Incense containing Star Anise may be placed on a Samhain altar, helping you to strengthen your connection to any visiting spirits.

Samhain Flowers

Flowers hold immense meaning to each of the eight sabbats that make up the Wheel of the Year. While their main function is often to serve as decoration for festivals, rituals, and altars, their placement is extremely significant, and will help to bring a sense of completion to Samhain festivities.

Periwinkle

Known in spiritualism as the Sorcerer's Violet and Flower of Immortality and of Death, the periwinkle has a long and storied history in the realm of the occult (Evert Hopman, 2021). The gray-purple flower is believed to be effective in warding off evil spirits and is often hung over doorways or placed on gateposts to repel any potential malevolence seeking entry. Periwinkle is also often worn on your person, helping you to evade negativity and evil as you move through your everyday life.

When using periwinkle for Samhain, these small charms could help guide only positive, familiar spirits towards houses and altars. Nowadays, a popular practice is to weave a wreath of periwinkle and place it on the door of the homestead. Beyond the protection provided by the flower, if you are looking to move from celebrating Samhain by yourself to participating in group rituals, the wreath could be instrumental in signaling to others that the inhabitants of the wreathed house are spiritualists. In addition to this, periwinkle can be included in the components of a Samhain altar if, during the sabbat, one of the deceased spirits being called and honored is that of a child. In the flower's lore, it is said that if periwinkle grows on or near the grave of a child, it could help the child's parents to sustain their spiritual connection to the departed.

Chrysanthemums

These bright autumnal flowers are often seen throughout decorations for both Samhain and Halloween. Oftentimes, chrysanthemums are placed on gravesites during the sabbat. They may also be incorporated into wreaths or placed on altars to aid with remembrance.

Thinking back to our first introduction to Samhain, we know that the sun and fire are two natural components that are extremely important to the festival, and celebrations are often centered around them. Chrysanthemums are closely associated with the sun, and using them in Samhain decorations and altars helps to keep the reverence for the star alive in modern celebrations. If you are unable to attend a Samhain bonfire or light one in your own home or area, chrysanthemums can be used to represent the element of fire, and will tie you and those you celebrate with more closely to the ancient roots of the festival.

Other Useful Plants

Vegetables for Samhain

While many modern-day Samhain and Halloween festivities involve carved pumpkins or turnips, we know that this practice dates back to pre-Christian Ireland. Jack O' Lanterns may be carved for the sabbat in honor of this ancient tradition. However, if you would like your celebration to resemble the Celtic practice more closely, once you have carved your pumpkin, turnip or beetroot, pour sand into the bottom of the hollowed-out space and place a candle into the grains. An inch of sand should suffice, but feel free to use your own judgment. On the night before Samhain, light the candle and place them in window sills or on your doorstep so that wandering spirits will know that they are welcome in the designated space.

Apples

The use of apples in Samhain rituals dates back to the Ancient Celtic celebrations of the sabbat. Apples are used most often in games of bobbing, as the spiritual properties mixed with those of the water are thought (Evert Hopman, 2021) to be able to bring participants closer to the supernatural realm and the Otherworld. If you would like to organize a game for your own festivities, make sure to pass a piece of silver through the water before beginning. While a pure silver coin would be most effective, silver jewelry would also work as an offering with which you can silver the water. Silvering helps to purify the water, readying it for ritualistic use. The use of silver to cleanse water is an age-old practice, as the metal is said to have significantly potent purifying qualities.

Apples may also be used for divination purposes. If you would like to set an intention of finding love in the new year, cut an apple into nine pieces just before twelve o'clock on the night of Samhain. Take these pieces into a darkened room and eat eight of the apple slices while looking into a mirror. Once you have finished the eighth slice, toss the ninth behind you while still looking into the mirror, for it is said that you will see the face of future love. Other amorous divinations that may be done using apples include tossing a fresh peel over your shoulder to reveal the initial of your soulmate's first names or giving an apple warmed by your hand to the object of your affections. In this latter ritual, it is said that if your feelings are reciprocated, they will bite into the apple.

Should your Samhain tastes skew away from love, or if you prefer strawberries over apples, you can use parts of the apple tree instead of the fruit. For Samhain purposes, build yourself a bell branch. This ritual item, which finds its origins in Druidic celebrations of the sabbat, is said to ward off negative and malevolent spirits while attracting fairies and other supernatural entities (Evert Hopman, 2021). Making a bell branch is incredibly simple, and could be used as a unifying exercise when done with members of a group celebrating Samhain together. Find yourself a piece of apple wood, or if it's sustainable, remove some directly from a living tree. Attach nine bells to the wood while keeping it clean of other adornments. Shake your bell branch before you begin any of your Samhain rituals, ensuring that any spirits or forces that would seek to sabotage your rite are expelled. With any luck, you might also be able to attract entities that could help you with the execution of a successful, powerful sabbat ritual.

Oak

At Samhain, when the worlds of the living and the dead are at their closest, it is important for us to honor those who have passed while still being observant of the time that lies ahead while we live. A balance must be struck between our reverence of the dead and our preparation for life, and oak is the perfect tree for this. Oak trees are regarded as symbolic of the equilibrium between worlds, as its branches stretch upwards toward life, while its roots reach down into the space that lies beneath (Evert Hopman, 2021). Oaks are said to be the gates to the Otherworld, and each tree contains a guardian spirit, making this particular plant immensely powerful when the veil between worlds thins.

When using oak during Samhain, our intentions must not only be that of balance, but also of protection. Find an oak tree near you and collect some of its fallen twigs. These twigs can then be fashioned into solar crosses, with both of the arms equal in length and bound together with a red string. If you carry this cross with you during the time of the sabbat or place it in doorways or windows, you will be granted protection from the malevolent spirits that visit alongside those we revere. If you would like to use the properties of the oak tree for the new year, collect some acorns and place them in your pockets. Set your intention for the abundance of creativity and inspiration, or if you are more family-minded, for fertility. Acorns may also be incorporated into the cakes baked for a dumb supper so that all those who eat this cake may enjoy protection. Logs from oak trees are also appropriate for use in ritual fires, so be on the lookout for them if you'd prefer to build your own Samhain bonfire, or if you are involved in the building of these fires for communal celebration.

Hawthorn

The hawthorn tree has been associated with the sabbat for centuries. It is often regarded as being similar to oak, in that both trees are said to function as gateways to worlds other than our own. Historically, hawthorn trees have been said to house fairies, and that any person wishing to see and interact with these entities will enjoy the most luck if they find themselves near a lone tree during Beltane, Midsummer or Samhain (Hawthorn & Honey, 2021). Should you wish to harvest the branches of this tree for use in Wheel of the Year celebrations, it is advised that you do so at Beltane. So, if you'd like to make hawthorn part of your Samhain rituals, you may need to do some planning in advance.

If, like many of us, planning ahead is not exactly your strong suit, don't worry, because hawthorn berries are in season and ripen around the time that Samhain is observed. After the berries have been harvested, you can make them into jams or dry them for use in tea. Using the fruit of the hawthorn tree in recipes for Samhain will bring your rituals closer to those of the Ancient Celts and enable an extra bit of otherworldly connection to the proceedings.

Rowan

Rowan wood occupies the same hallowed, ancient space as oak and hawthorn, with ritualistic usage of the wood dating back centuries, all the way to the Ancient Celts. Rowan holds a strong connection to the dead, its most common use being to act as a deterrent for any deceased people (Hawthorn & Honey, 2021) who might be looking to rise up on nights other than Samhain. It is for this purpose that rowan bushes are often planted in cemeteries.

When using the rowan plant for Samhain rituals, your intention must guide you towards protection. Hanging rowan branches and berries around your homestead will allow you to filter through all the spirits who are out-and-about on Samhain night, enabling you to invite only the kind ones into your home. If you don't have access to the branches, rowan berries can be incorporated into a wreath or garland, perhaps alongside periwinkle. Hanging this wreath on your door will keep your home free of any unwanted, ill-intentioned visitors from the Otherworld.

Samhain Crystals

The types of natural materials that bear importance during Samhain extend beyond the floral kingdom. When celebrating the sabbat, spiritual and metaphysical help and guidance may be obtained through the use of crystals (Booth, 2018). There are a number of crystals that will prove to be effective during the festival, though it is important to note that none of their properties will work quite right if the stones are not cleansed and charged in the correct manner. Before using your crystals for Samhain, remember to set your intention, preferably one that is in line with the properties of the crystal. Finally, remember that you do not need to use all of the crystals listed below. After reading this section, go to a merchant near you and seek out the crystals listed here. If they feel right, consider buying them for use during Samhain. If not, move on to the next.

Obsidian

We kick off our crystalline exploration with something that is, somewhat ironically, not a crystal. Obsidian is in fact a type of volcanic glass. Nevertheless, this stone possesses a great deal of power, and its effects may be especially potent at the time of the sabbat.

Obsidian is an excellent divinatory tool, and if you would like to take a stab at scrying on Samhain, be sure to include this crystal among your tools. In addition to this, obsidian may help you with any grounding work you seek to do during the sabbat. Grounding is important for Samhain, as we must be attuned to our natural world before we can travel into the spaces of another.

Smokey Quartz

Another crystal that is an effective tool for grounding, smokey quartz will not only help you to ground yourself, but will also aid you in anchoring any spiritual energy you may encounter during a ritual. Smokey quartz grounds you by unlocking your Root Chakra, so feel free to add some chakra work into any rituals involving this stone, the effects would be dazzlingly strong. Additionally, this crystal extends a barrier of protection, helping you to keep your metaphysical interactions limited to the more friendly spirits (*The best crystals for Samhain*, 2022). Smokey quartz may also prove helpful in leveling the playing field between you and spiritual visitors by bringing the latter party down to your own level of psychic perception. Not only will this make it easier to establish initial contact with the spirits, but it will also facilitate a much easier and smoother flow of communication.

Amethyst

Though used today as an introductory stone by most crystal enthusiasts, amethyst has a connection to ritualistic practice that goes back several centuries. The frequency at which this stone vibrates and operates is relatively high (Neshevich, 2020), and as such, it possesses quite a few remarkable capabilities. The first among these is the strength amethyst can put towards protecting its user. During Samhain rituals, it would be wise to keep an amethyst crystal on your person so that you may comfortably perform your rites from inside the space of protection the stone will create around you. The protection provided by amethyst will ensure that you avoid any malevolent spirits, but it will also protect you from any energies that would seek to interfere with your own.

Selenite

Another vibrationally potent stone, selenite is most often employed for healing and energy. When used during Samhain, however, the selenite stone can help you to quiet and clear your mind so that you may commune with spirits more easily.

Black Tourmaline

This dark stone may also be used to protect us and our companions during the sabbat. Black tourmaline is nearly as strong as amethyst in expelling and warding off negative spirits and energies. The stone could also be helpful in the time leading up to

Samhain, and even in the new year that follows it. Black tourmaline is known to have quite potent cleansing properties, and may be just what you need to leave any negativity or internal conflict in the cycle that expires (*The best crystals for Samhain*, 2022).

A great many plants and crystals are associated with and used for the festival of Samhain. While their uses range from divination to strengthening fertility to finding the love of your life, many of them perform the task of keeping you safe. Understandably, this might sound incredibly easy and slightly underwhelming, as there are far more wondrous and mystical things than protection. True as this might be, when it comes to Samhain and the time we spend communing with spirits and entities that are different from and potentially stronger than us, there is nothing more important than retaining a barrier of safeguarding.

This chapter provided you with many options to choose from when preparing for and executing your Samhain rituals. When selecting your materials, you must remember that there is no set, specific way in which you have to celebrate Samhain. If you're a fan of periwinkle, use it as much as you want. If you've never really come to love chrysanthemums, leave them out of your decorations. Regardless of the point of view from which you are celebrating the sabbat, what is most important is that you choose the rights, rituals, and components that will serve you best, and that will give you the most comfortable, most revelatory experiences. Make it your own, for there is no way you could go wrong.

Key Takeaways

- The first and best place to look for the components that make up the perfect Samhain is the great outdoors. There you will find all of the herbs, flowers, fruits, vegetables, and even crystals you need to enjoy the best version of the festival possible.

- Some herbs that are associated with the festival of Samhain include rosemary, mugwort, and star anise. These herbs will help you in acts of remembrance, strengthen your connection to the spirits of the Otherworld, and make the process of communicating with them significantly easier.

- The periwinkle and chrysanthemum flowers are used during Samhain. The former is a powerful protective talisman and symbol of remembrance for deceased children. The latter flower is used in Samhain decorations and, while they also act as an aid of remembrance, they hold symbolic significance and will represent the sun and the primal element of fire in your Samhain festivities.

- Other plants that you may find useful at the time of the sabbat include pumpkins, turnips, beetroot, apples, as well as the wood, fruit, and seeds of the oak and hawthorn trees and the rowan bush.

- Crystals that will prove effective when used for Samhain are obsidian, smokey quartz, amethyst, selenite, and black tourmaline. These stones will help to ground you, will sharpen your psychic abilities, and will protect you from any malevolence that might seek you out on the night of Samhain.

- While there are many natural materials that may be used during celebrations of Samhain, it is important to remember that all of them do not need to be used, and that it is more than alright if you choose to make use of only those materials that speak to your sensibilities, values, and spiritualist practice.

CHAPTER 6:

Samhain Structures – The Altar

> *An ancestor altar is a sacred space that honors your deceased loved ones and can be used for prayers, offerings, and spells.*
> –Michelle Gruben

Along with the ancient beliefs, rituals, and calendrical shakeup that constitutes Samhain come a few other things that have become sabbat staples. The Samhain altar is as old as the festival itself, and all of those items and tools we associate most with the Ancient Celtic New Year can be found on these structures. In this chapter, we will explore the meaning behind the Samhain altar and will discover how we can go about selecting the materials for our altars before we learn how to make these places of veneration ourselves.

The Samhain Altar

Altars have been built and used for Samhain since time immemorial. Before the festival came to include ancestral observances, when it existed solely as a harvest festival and annual an demarcator, people built altars and populated them with things significant to the season, the year that was ending, and the year that was edging over the horizon.

In the early days of the festival, stone and wooden altars were constructed and decorated with items from the last harvest (Smith, 2019). Because the winter began with the sabbat, and the harvest season had come to an end, gourds, grains, and other fruits and vegetables were placed on altars as a means of giving thanks for the agricultural prosperity the community had enjoyed, and to petition the deities (at the time, Pagan and Druidic) to renew this prosperity when the time came to harvest again. The altars of the Ancient Celtic people were mainly seasonal, and included items that represented the colors of the season. As such, these altars were decorated with items in a variety of oranges, reds, and yellows. Not only were these items and colors symbolic of the change of seasons, but they were also used, alongside candles, to connect the altar to the sun and the element of fire. Both the sun and fire (do Nascimento, 2020) are incredibly important to Samhain, as we are well aware by now. By representing them on the altar, ancient celebrators could bring their structure full circle and have an embodiment of the entire festival in front of them.

Over time, as the festival evolved and came to include ancestral veneration in a more significant capacity, so did the altars. This evolution endured over time, and eventually overtook the harvest and seasonal sections of Samhain altars. Modern-day celebrations mainly focus on the use of altars for honoring, contacting, and communicating with the spirits of our deceased ancestors. Despite this difference in purpose, many of the original components of the Samhain altars are still used to this day (do Nascimento, 2020). Now, if harvest items or those representing the sun are incorporated into a Samhain altar, it serves to connect the ritualistic use of the altar to its Ancient Celtic roots. That being said, many Wiccan and Neo-Pagan celebrants do hold the same beliefs regarding the sun and the elements as their pre-Christian counterparts.

Modern Samhain altars tend to focus more on the ancestral aspect of the sabbat (Gruben, 2022). These altars, while still characterized by the seasonal and harvest aspect, now mainly include items and tools that will enable you to contact, communicate with, and honor your ancestors. We will explore what is placed on ancestral altars later on, but it is important to be aware that the construction and use of an ancestral altar is an incredibly personal thing. As such, a lot of care and thought must be placed into the items you will use to make your altar, their placement, as well as how they will be used when the altar is active. Ancestral altars serve as places of observance and respect, where you can go when the veil has thinned to be with the ones you love but cannot ordinarily be close to. Altars are the first place where you will meet the spirits of your deceased loved ones, and they are the structures that will alert these spirits of your veneration, inviting them to come and commune with you.

Whether you use a Samhain altar to mark the passing of the seasons and the beginning of a new cycle or to feel close to the people you have loved and lost, its importance remains the same. If you are celebrating Samhain, it is wise to plan the undertaking of a variety of rituals and celebrations. However, before any of that can be done, you must build your altar so that you are ready to worship, give thanks, call down, or spend a moment in silent remembrance. Samhain begins with your altar.

Building the Samhain Altar

Before we look at the different components that make up a Samhain altar and how they may be put together, we need to understand that personalization is key at every stage of this construction. When selecting your materials, building your altar, and eventually making use of it, the main focus has to be what you want to get from the altar. If you would like to, set an intention before you begin to gather your altar materials. This will help guide you towards making the right selection, and will simplify the building process. Once you begin to use your altar, remember your intention, as this will help you to correctly and safely utilize it. If you would like to commune with the spirits of deceased family members or friends, keep this in mind throughout the entire process. The same principle counts if you are building a Samhain altar for the purpose of thanksgiving.

Selecting Materials

Samhain altars may be made up of an array of items, each of which will have a different meaning or representation. While we will look at those items that are most often incorporated into these altars, it is important to note that this section will serve only as a guideline, and that you must choose only the items with which you feel most comfortable and which suit your needs best.

We will begin building the altar from the bottom upwards, so why not begin our material selection there as well? Your altar must be covered with a cloth, and most people choose a dark cloth (usually black) (do Nascimento, 2020) which will lay the foundation for the ancestral connection. If you would like your altar to also invoke or be connected to the autumnal season, feel free to choose cloths in the color of the season. Choose colors such as red, yellow, orange or purple.

Now that we have our base layer selected, let's move on to what will be placed on top of our cloth. It is here that your intuition must come strongly into play, allowing you to choose only those items to which you feel some sort of connection or pull. As Samhain altars are mainly ancestral nowadays, we begin by selecting symbols of your ancestors. These can be photographs or items that belonged to them that you still cherish. The common practice is to build an ancestral altar for our grandparents and great-grandparents, but if you like to include generations that are further back or even closer to your own, feel free to do so. Seeing as the main purpose of the altar is to commune with spirits of the deceased, note that you needn't limit yourselves to your blood relatives. If you have friends or members of a chosen family who have passed on and with whom you would like to connect on Samhain, include them on your altar. The same principle is in effect for deceased children. Though we call them ancestral altars, they are conduits for spirits of all ages and degrees of relation.

Next up on our Samhain checklist is iconography of death. Symbols of death that are the easiest to find in stores are those of skulls, skeletons (*How to set up a Gorgeous Samhain Altar*, 2021), and a scythe-wielding Grim Reaper. That being said, if you have a knack for crafts, feel free to create your own talismans from clay, grass, sand, or other natural materials. If your religious worship includes a deity of death and the afterlife, you can include a statue or religious object associated with them in their honor.

Once you have gathered all your deathly items, you can begin to look for tools of divination you would like to use at your altar. Even if divination isn't exactly your strong suit, it might be advisable to keep some of these items on the altar, as they will help you to make contact with the spirits much more easily. Popular divination tools include tarot cards, scrying glasses and mirrors, runes, and crystal balls. When gathering your tools, you may want to quickly page back to Chapter 5 where we explored the different types of crystals that work best during Samhain. You will find that a number of them will help you to divine more easily, as well as strengthen your spiritual connection.

Finally, the last of your materials may be sourced from symbols of the final harvest. Typically, the last harvest of the year is represented on the altar by food items that were obtained in this last reaping. Popular harvest food items include pumpkins and gourds, apples, and corn. If your geographical region or religious teachings allow for other crops to be harvested before Samhain, you can include these in your altar. Though the harvest is typically recognized through the use of edible things, you can also honor the fertile soil by using a cornucopia. People have been known to include some of the farm tools they used during the harvest, so if you have these at hand, why not add them to the pile?

If you would like, you can also add some herbs and incense (see Chapter 5) to add an aromatherapeutic aspect to your Samhain altar. If not, the selection of your altar materials should now be complete. At this point in time, I would suggest spending some time with the items you have chosen. Make sure that you truly feel some sort of connection to them, and that you haven't simply selected them so that your altar looks more populated. Remember that the weaker your connection to the talismans on your altar, the weaker your connection to the ancestral spirits.

Constructing an Altar

Now that you have all the ingredients you need, let's get working on your altar.

Before we can begin putting anything together, we have to determine where our altar will be placed. Samhain altars can be built on a variety of things, but the only requirement is that the foundational structure be stable, given the number of open flames that may be on it at any given time (do Nascimento, 2020). Most people opt for a table or shelf, but you can use your mantle or any other place that feels right. The altar will be your most important point of contact for the entirety of the sabbat. As such, make sure that you select a space where you will be able to have a moment's peace, where you can reflect and become attuned with the spiritual currents of Samhain. In addition to this, you must build your altar in a place that grants it the respect and honor that it deserves. What this means is that while it would be perfectly fine to construct your altar on a designated table in the family room, you would do well to steer clear of the garage when searching for altar spaces.

Once you have found the perfect place for your ancestral altar, start building it from the basal layer upwards. Begin by laying down your cloth. If you have selected multiple cloths in multiple colors, lay down the black cloth first. This should be the largest of the cloths on which you can place the smaller, seasonally-colored ones.

Next, your ancestral talismans. If you have chosen photographs of your ancestors, place them in the most prominent spot, with any other items that belonged to or that you associate with them arranged around their portraits. If you are honoring ancestors on both sides of your family, designate space on the altar for each one. Have the two familial branches meet in the middle of your altar. If you are not dedicating your altar to any specific sections of your family, arrange the ancestral talismans any way you see fit.

Place candles among the items representing your ancestors. Most practitioners choose white candles for the invitation of kind and benevolent spirits (Gruben, 2022), but if you would like to add some autumnal flair at this stage, you can use candles in the colors of the season. Another popular choice of candle color is black, said to represent and pay tribute to the Mighty Dead.

Your visual sense has already been engaged, and now it is time for your olfactory sense to be awakened by your altar. Place incense, flowers, and fragrant herbs on your altar. Some of these aromatic items will help you to honor nature, something that plays a crucial role in the time leading up to and following Samhain. Others will strengthen your connection to your ancestral spirits. If you are looking to provide the spirits with an enjoyably-scented journey to this realm, consider using sandalwood, rose, or frankincense. Alternatively, you can use rosemary and sage for remembrance, as well as myrrh and rue for grief. Alongside these scented items, you can incorporate your harvest symbols into your altar. Remember to choose crops that were obtained during the final harvest before Samhain. Even if you do not hold any particular fondness for harvests, including these items will help you to connect to the original seasonal Samhain.

We move on to our symbols and talismans of death. If you have made skulls or skeletons from clay, or have drawn an illustration of the Grim Reaper, place these on your altar now. If you'd like, include some statuary representing the deity of death in your particular religious canon. While the purpose of the altar is to get in touch with entities residing in the Otherworld, be mindful not to let the presence of death on your altar become too overwhelming.

Finally, for the finishing touch, place your tools of divination on the altar. Keep in mind that when you begin using your altar to call down and make contact with your ancestral spirits, you might need to use these tools. As such, be careful not to bury them too deep. Keep them near the front, somewhere that they are still visible without being the thing that draws your eye to the altar. If you are not a diviner yourself, don't discount these items, as their presence may very well strengthen your ancestral connection just enough for you to commune with those who have passed.

Making Use of Your Altar

Naturally, the purpose of an ancestral altar is to bring you into contact with the spirits of your forebears. Whether you are new to this practice or have been performing ancestral rituals for some time, a good place to start is with reflection and prayer. Go to your altar and light a candle (you can light more, but if you are communing with one ancestor in particular, one should suffice). Sit before your altar and reflect on the significance of your ancestor's life before your birth. Think of what they mean to you now, and think of the way in which you would like them to guide you in the future. Once your reflection is complete, turn your thoughts into prayer. Either silently or out loud, cast your prayer toward your altar and feel yourself connect with your ancestor. Stay before your altar as long as you need, until you feel the connection fade away.

During the festival of Samhain, spend time at your altar whenever you can. Pray to or commune with your ancestors and any other spirits you would like to connect with and honor. If you observe a religion with deities presiding over the harvest and the realms of death respectively, honor them with your altar. It can be as simple as lighting a candle and thanking them for the year that has passed and the prosperity you have enjoyed. Conversely, you can ask them for blessings and guidance as you enter a new cycle, both of the calendar and in your life.

When using the altar to contact your ancestors for purposes other than praying, you will also begin by lighting a candle. Before we delve further into the ritual, note that the same approach may be taken should you wish to invoke other supernatural or metaphysical entities you have honored on your altar. After lighting the candle, call their name out loud. If your purpose in summoning them is for them to partake in a Samhain dumb supper, state your intention clearly in the form of a wish. Should you merely be invoking them for the purpose of providing them with offerings, place the offering on the altar. Stay at the altar until you feel the spirit has been sated, or as long as you are comfortable. If you are providing offerings of food and drink throughout Samhain, be sure to replenish them on a daily basis. Day-old sacraments must preferably be discarded in nature, but if your local ecology does not allow for this, dispose of them with the rest of your domestic waste.

Let these rituals serve only as a guideline for using your altar. The way in which you construct and make use of your altar is entirely up to you. Only you know what the true purpose of the altar is, and what you hope to gain from its use. Do not attempt rituals with which you are uncomfortable. Once Samhain has passed, take down your altar piece by piece and store all the components in a designated box where they will remain, ready for use at the end of the next cycle.

Key Takeaways

- Samhain altars are essential for the proper celebration of the sabbat, as they provide us with spaces where we can give thanks, both for the harvest and for the impact that our ancestors have had on our lives.

- Ancestor altars are compiled using cloths in the colors of Samhain, usually black, with cloths in the colors of the season on top. In addition to this, ancestral talismans, candles, harvest items, death iconography, divinatory tools, and scented items are added to round out the different components of the altar.

- Altars should be built in spaces where users can take moments of prayer, reflection, and celebrations.

- When building the altar, start with the cloth, adding the ancestral talismans, then the candles, scented and harvest items, symbols of death, finally placing your tools of divination on the altar. Arrange your components in the way that makes the most sense to you.

- When using your altar, begin by lighting a candle and saying a prayer to the spirits being honored there. You can also light a candle and take time to reflect.

- When calling down the spirits represented on the altar, light a candle before invoking their names. Offerings always help. If your offerings are edible, replace them daily and dispose of the old items responsibly.

- Once Samhain has passed, carefully disassemble your altar and pack it away securely for the next time the sabbat comes around.

CHAPTER 7:

Celebrating Samhain—Spells

As I light this candle, / I bid the Old Year farewell, / With gratitude for milestones passed, / And memories cherished. / And I welcome the New Year in / With love and warmth and blessings. –Janina Renée

During Samhain, there are a myriad of ways in which we can celebrate the sabbat. One of these ways is to take advantage of the spiritual energy that is heightened at the time of the festival, and we do so by casting spells. This chapter will explore how spells fit into Samhain festivities, and will provide you with some invocations you can use yourself in order to capitalize on the metaphysical potential of the sabbat.

Samhain Spells

Spells have always been a part of Samhain, due in large part to the great influx of magical energy that our world experiences during the time of the sabbat. Using spells as part of Samhain rituals has long helped people to prepare for the New Year, bid farewell to the one that falls away, as well as receive guidance from their ancestors regarding the time that lies ahead (Tremeer, 2021).

When moving through this chapter, as well as when implementing its guidance during the sabbat, it is essential to remember what happens when you cast a spell. When performing this type of rite, you are communicating directly to the universe, as well as to your own mind and spirit. You are declaring your hopes and intentions to each of these things, and regardless of the nature or effects of your spell, you are making the decision to move your life in a particular direction. You must also keep in mind that when you cast a spell, you are asking the universe for the ability to harness and mold its energies into the things you wish to bring about.

This is why spells are so often used during Samhain, as the universe brings its metaphysical and magical energies closer to our world at this time. Spells invoked during Samhain tend to focus on the beginning of a new cycle, aiming for the individual to experience some type of change or improvement. In the following section, we will be looking at some spells that may be used for health, guidance, and prosperity. These are common things to desire at Samhain, as the promise of a new year and a clean slate brings endless possibilities.

Your Own Invocations

Before reading the spells below, keep in mind that for any of your invocations to work, each individual spell requires five basic tenets: intent, desire, focus, release, and belief. If any one of these elements is missing, you will be doing nothing more than speaking empty words to even emptier air.

Spell Jars

If you are looking to use spells as part of your Samhain observance, then chances are that you've made some incantations before. However, if this is your first time invoking things of any kind, a spell jar is an easy way to introduce yourself to the practice. Regardless of your degree of competence or experience with spell-casting, spell jars always come in handy, and many seasoned pros make use of them.

Besides functioning as an introductory experience, spell jars are also excellent ways to channel your intention and subsequent magic into a more concentrated and potent form. Moreover, if this is your first time casting, you might find it difficult to visualize your spell as a coherent concept (Anuwen, 2021). Spell jars help with this, as they enable you to see all the different components of your spell simultaneously, which in turn helps you to picture your incantation taking effect. Before we begin putting together our first witch bottle, it's worth mentioning that while the majority can be built in and enacted from these containers, spells aren't always one-size-fits-all. While some may contain enough of the common components needed to make a spell jar, others will involve fewer materials and may not warrant such a jar at all.

Before building your spell jar, clear your space, both physically and energetically. Since we will be working with lit candles, make sure there is nothing in the area surrounding your jar that could become kindling. Additionally, by clearing the energy of the space, you can begin building your spell surrounded by fresh and clean energy.

First things first: gather your materials. You will need a jar, preferably one made of glass that can be sealed. Next, select a candle. The color of the candle is very important, and will vary between spells (for instance, red candles are used for love spells, whereas white candles will be best suited to spells for the New Year). Add a piece of paper and a pen to the pile, along with the herbs needed for your spell (if you are performing a New Year's spell, use something tied to remembrance, like rosemary or periwinkle). Finally, select the crystals you will use during your spell (again, these will differ depending on the type of spell being cast).

Once you have gathered all your materials, cleanse them. Using clean components in a clean space will make for the most potent incantation. When you've done this, take a moment to examine the things you have chosen, as well as the spell you are attempting to cast. Set your intention, visualize exactly how you would like your spell to take effect, how you wish for it to affect your own life, as well as that of those around you. Take as much time as you need to zero in on your exact intention, and try to condense it into one sentence. Once you have determined your sentence, write it on the piece of paper. If your practice involves runic work, include some sigils on your paper for good measure. Drop your paper into your jar, allowing it to form the bottom-most layer.

Next, take up your herbs and place them inside the jar, covering your intention paper. After your herbal layer, add your chosen crystals. They can either be whole stones or smaller crystalline fragments. The size doesn't matter as much as the strength of your intention and belief. If you have brought other materials to use that you feel align with and strengthen your spell, add them into the jar on top of the crystals. Though we are talking about the different 'layers' of your witch bottle, the components needn't lay on separate levels, so don't panic if they mix.

Finally, light your candle and allow the wax to drip over the jar. Enough wax has to drip over the lid for you to be able to seal the jar with it. Let the candle wax drip over the sides of the jar as well, coating the sides generously. While you coat your jar, if you'd like, you can chant your intention in order to strengthen the effects of the spell. Once you have waxed the jar to your satisfaction, you can either extinguish the candle or allow it to burn further. The latter is advisable, as you are performing candle magic, and the longer the flame lasts, the stronger you make your incantation.

All that's left now is to place your spell jar in a prominent place. Choose a spot that allows you to see the jar on a regular basis. Every time that you move past it, you will be reminded of your intention, helping you replenish its energy.

Spells for the New Year

As Samhain marks the end of one annual cycle and the beginning of another, it stands to reason that spells focused on the months to come will be especially potent during the sabbat.

New Year's Welcoming Spell

The first New Year's spell you can attempt is a simple form of candle magic, and does not require any extensive preparation or very many components. The only thing you need is a white candle. On the eve of Samhain, right before the New Year begins at midnight, invoke the recitation below. If you are unable to perform the spell at midnight, try to get as close as you can before the year changes over. You are also able to cast this spell at any point during the day on November 1st, but be sure to cast it on the first day of the New Year. This spell can be cast individually or in groups. When casting, adapt the singular and plural pronouns accordingly.

SAMHAIN

Light your candle and recite the following, noting that you may change the thanksgivings, wishes, and hopes to suit your purposes:

The tides of this year have changed for the final time,

The clock of this cycle has entered its final hour.

As the final knells ring out,

I look back with gratitude

With love

With awareness.

At this point, pause your verbal incantation and reflect on the year that has passed. Think of all its events and aspects, both good and bad. Release each past occurrence, keeping only their effects. Return to the spell.

A cycle begins anew

And with it, the potential for a life renewed.

For the assurance of this renewal,

I see the year before me.

I see abundance,

I see light and love,

I see happiness.

I empower my words and my actions

To bring these changes into my life,

And I wrap my hopes and wishes

In the light of newness

That we may find one another with ease

In the time to come.

Place your lit candle on your Samhain altar and allow the energy of your spell to flow a while longer. Do this by either allowing the candle to burn continuously until it is melted entirely or by relighting it each day to revitalize your magic. Do not worry about how long the flame lasts, as your incantation will provide you with light for the entire year.

A Spell for the Future

When the New Year begins, another popular type of spell is one used to gain a measure of control over the time that lies ahead. This spell involves visualization and manifestation. Note that, once again, you can personalize this spell any way you want.

First, find a quiet space where you can calm and quiet down. Once you have cleared your mind of all cumbersome thoughts, cast your mind and heart to the future. Imagine the timeline of your life. This timeline can be vast, covering the rest of your time on Earth, or it can be short-term, looking only at the year that lies ahead. Regardless of the period covered, visualize your life during it. Try to see as much as you can, down to the minutiae.

Now, write this timeline down in your spellbook or on a piece of paper, whichever is more convenient. Write down everything you saw, exactly as you remember it. Take the book or paper containing your timeline and place it on your Samhain altar. If you'd like, you can make a spell jar and store your timeline inside. Once it has a place on the altar, call upon your ancestral spirits to help you learn from your past and move away from the future you don't want, towards the one to which you aspire. Leave this timeline on the altar as long as it is up. If you pack away your altar after Samhain, place the spell paper in a prominent place, and make sure that you are reminded of your goals and intentions whenever you see it.

A Spell for Guidance

When Samhain rolls around, people often want to ask for guidance, be it from ancestral spirits, the universe, or any of the benevolent supernatural entities that abound during this time, be they your guardian angel or spirit guide. The following spell will help you to ask for this guidance, and given that it is a sigil spell, it will be relatively easy to cast.

Begin the incantation by calling down the spirit or entity from whom you would like to receive guidance. If you have other methods of doing this, you can use your Samhain altar.

You will be using your spell book for the next step. If you do not have a spell book, any paper you have at hand will work just fine. Write down what you are seeking guidance for. Try to be as concise as possible. If what you are struggling with can be captured in one word, use one word only. Next, review what you have written and cross out any vowels, as well as letters that repeat. Take the letters you are left with and rearrange them into a sigil. The shape or sequence should feel right and personal.

Activate your sigil by means of breath. You can do this any way you like, whether through screaming, chanting, singing, etc. The choice is yours. Once activated, hold your sigil close to your heart and imbue it with the power of your intention, as well as the energy you have called forth to cast this spell.

The next step involves burning your sigil. If you would prefer not to, place it somewhere safe. You may also use a spell jar here.

Regardless of your method, distance yourself from the sigil, and release yourself from the weight of the intention. Once you have done away with your sigil, remove it and the intention from your mind. Thank your invoked power for their help and release them as well. Move on with your life and wait for the guidance to come.

A Spell for Health

Samhain is a time for change and improvement, and one thing that people often seek to improve in the New Year is their health, both mental and physical.

Before you begin casting, you will need to cleanse the space in which you will work. Choose a smudging herb that you feel will suit your intention the best. If you are unsure which herb to use, default to sage, as it will help you clear the space of any negative energy that might interfere with your healing. After cleansing, find a piece of paper and a pen, and if you have it, a clear quartz crystal (the stone is optional, but may strengthen the incantation).

Find a spot on the floor, or anywhere you feel comfortable and able to meditate. Tune out the sounds of the world around you. Focus on your breath and follow it as it fills every part of your body. Take a deep breath and follow its path to the afflicted part of your body; if you feel pain there, do not shy away from it, but acknowledge its existence. Examine this pain, feel its intensity. Take another breath in and visualize your body without that pain. Remember how you felt before and think of how you will feel after.

On your piece of paper, write down the details of your ailment. Be specific and provide adequate details while also keeping it brief. Look at your writing and feel the connection you have to the words describing what ails you. Next, underneath this description, write how you will be healed. Write what will happen once your wound (whether physical or emotional) has closed over, and how your heart and body will feel. Finally, underneath these two sections, write your spell. This can be an affirmation of your healing, or simply the words "So mote it be." Choose a phrase or two that reinforces your belief in the healing process.

You can take this piece of paper and carry it with you until you have healed fully, allowing it to remind you of your intention. Alternatively, tear off the section describing the illness and burn it, releasing the ailment. Keep the healing process and spell with you until the cure has taken effect.

Though this spell can be used solely for the purpose of healing, it is worth noting that some of the other spells covered in this chapter could also be adapted to bring about healing. Look for those that have you write an intention or describe the effects of the spell, and alter them to suit your healing needs.

A Spell for Prosperity

We conclude this chapter with a spell commonly invoked during the sabbat, one that appeals to the forces of the universe to grant us good fortune and a prosperous future (Coughlin, 2018). Though this particular spell is most often employed with the intention of experiencing some kind of windfall, its basic tenets are those of a reversal of fortune and of the individual flourishing. With this in mind, adapt the spell as you will.

To cast this spell, you will need some sage or other herbs used for smudging, a pen, and a bay leaf. The bay leaf is the most important component, as it is an incredibly powerful talisman of fortune. Its inclusion in this spell is sure to have you thriving all year round.

Before you begin working with your bay leaf, cleanse the area in which you will be casting. This is a crucial step in the process, as you are asking the universe to clean the slate of your luck, so you need a clean, energetic space to do so.

After cleansing the space, take your bay leaf and, using your pen, write your wish on the leaf. Naturally, a leaf does not have space for paragraphs of writing, but make sure that you include the specific type of prosperity you wish to enjoy (financial, emotional, romantic, etc.). While you are writing, focus all of your attention and energy on your wish. Put the full weight of your intentional capabilities into inscribing that leaf.

Let the ink dry. While it does, gaze at your wish, reinforcing your intention and reassuring the universe of your strong desire and need. Once the ink has dried entirely, set your leaf ablaze. As you watch the flames, visualize your spell, along with your wish, shooting out from the space around you, traveling to the furthest corners of this realm and every one beyond it. Once the leaf has been incinerated entirely, put the thought from your mind and let the universe work its magic.

In this chapter, we have covered only a few of the types of spells that people use during Samhain. There are many more incantations that are cast during the sabbat, and you should explore these and find the ones that will help you fulfill your individual needs and grant your wishes. As always, remember to adapt each spell until it feels right for you.

Key Takeaways

- Spells make up an important part of Samhain festivities, helping people to prepare for the year that lies ahead, as well as make use of the heightened metaphysical power present during the sabbat.

- An easy way to introduce yourself to the world of spell-casting is by making spell jars. By adding spell components layer-by-layer, you can see what goes into your incantation and how all of the different parts interact.

- Spells for the New Year often focus on giving thanks for the time that has passed, while also asking for blessings and positivity in the months that lie ahead.

- By using future spells during Samhain, you can gain some control over the year before it has even begun.

- Spells for guidance and prosperity are also commonly used during Samhain. Not only do these spells function within the New Year's context of the festival, but also allow practitioners to call upon their ancestral spirits to help and guide them as they move forward in life.

CHAPTER 8:
Celebrating Samhain— Rituals

> *Across these three days and nights, death was embraced as a natural part of life, and people let the spirits wash over them with respect, receptivity and celebration.* –Grace McGrade

Ritual practice forms an integral part of the celebration of Samhain, and the rites carried out by celebrators often serve to make the festival accessible. In this chapter, we will explore the significance of rituals as a part of Samhain, as well as a few rituals you will be able to implement the next time the New Year rolls around.

The Rites of Samhain

For as long as people have celebrated Samhain, there have been rituals for observing the sabbat. In the first few chapters of this book, we looked at the different ways in which the Ancient Celtic Pagans and Druids celebrated this seasonal festival. Back then, rituals were centered around the veneration of nature and the giving of thanks to the higher powers that ensured the arrival of a plentiful harvest. Over time, as Samhain evolved and came to include the ancestral spirits of the community, the rituals evolved along with them. From this evolution came the building and use of ancestor altars as well as the casting of spells appealing to the powers of our forebears' spirits.

In modern iterations of the sabbat, ritual celebrations tend to lean more into this last, most recent aspect of Samhain. Most people who observe Samhain focus their rituals around communicating with and honoring their ancestors. Given the modern tendency to customize celebrations, many people choose to incorporate aspects of nature into their ancestral rituals, while others opt for only engaging with the natural world at the time of the sabbat.

Though Samhain celebrations have diverged somewhat into those focused on the dead and those focused on the natural world (Wood, 2021), one thing that unifies people of both camps is the use of food in rituals. As we will see in a minute, food features prominently in Samhain rites, whether used as an offering for a dumb supper or in a ritual giving thanks for a robust harvest.

However you choose to celebrate Samhain, whichever way your inclination leans, the fact remains that you cannot observe the sabbat without performing at least one ritual. With rituals being as effective as they are, chances are that once you've performed your first rite, you will soon find yourself eagerly joining in others, eventually building up an entire ritualistic Samhain itinerary.

Performing Your Own Rituals

In this section, we will be looking at three different types of Samhain rituals: séances, feasts, and time in the great outdoors. These are the rituals most commonly performed in honor of the festival, but there are many more that may also prove appropriate for this time of year. As with the spells and altars, feel free to change the specifics of the rituals to suit your own personal Samhain setup.

Séances

Before we begin detailing this ritual, it is important to note that the word 'séance' is being used as a catch-all term representing any type of ancestral ritual executed during Samhain. Rituals such as these involve the establishment of some type of connection between you and the spiritual world, and some may even require you to journey there to call forth the ancestral spirits with whom you want to convene.

Enter the Otherworld

Begin your journey by finding a quiet and calm space. Assume a resting position, as if you were about to begin a meditation. Take up mindful breathing, focusing on the power you use for inhalation and exhalation. Close your eyes and cast your mind to a place of transition. If you can, attempt to enter a liminal space that is connected to your past in some way.

Enter this place and move across its open expanse. As you approach the end of the space, visualize a place that you can connect to your heritage, be it cultural, ethnic or religious. Imagine now that, as you reach this place of ancestral welcome, the spirit of a forebear waits for you. Greet this spirit, provide them with an offering and thank them for their willingness to guide you. Once this initial contact has been made, you are free to commune with your spirit guide. Ask them questions, explore their stories and wisdom. Stay on this plane for as long as you need and for as long as you feel safe. When it is time to go, thank your ancestor once more and take your journey in reverse, coming back to yourself in this realm.

A Ritual for Local Spirits

Though we tend to focus only on our ancestral spirits during Samhain, we mustn't ignore the multitude of other ghostly wanderers that populate the world during the sabbat, especially in the spaces that we regularly inhabit.

This ritual begins with the building of a Samhain altar, which you will already have done. Ensure that your altar is prepared for a ritual, lighting any candles you have that facilitate spiritual communion. Additionally, gather leaves, sticks, flowers, and herbs from your local environment and mix them together to create a brew. Keep this brew for later in the ritual.

Contact the spirits in your space by providing them with an offering. This offering can consist of natural foods, items that represent your locality placed on the altar, or even a simple-yet-sweet incense. Whatever your offering is, set it in the space you have designated for spiritual contact and darken the entirety of your home.

Next, draw a warm bath and add the brew you made prior to the start of this ritual. If you cannot draw a full bath, add this brew to lukewarm water and pour it over your head. When using either method, after dousing yourself in the water, make sure not to dry yourself off too thoroughly. Also note that any light used during this part of the ritual must come only from a candle. After bathing, approach your altar (if you prefer to be dressed, ensure that the clothes you don are clean). Light the candles and incense on your altar and feel yourself sink back into the darkness of the room.

Find a place for yourself in that darkness, one where you feel safe and in control. Once you are in this space, speak your intention to the gathered spirits. Let the spirits know what you hope to gain from connecting with them, as well as how you desire this relationship to proceed. Ask any questions you feel are pertinent, and do not be afraid to get to know the spirits. If you find that you have nothing to say beyond your intention, you can sit in silence and simply co-exist.

You will feel when it is time to go. When this moment arrives, you can make another offering to end the ritual, or you can simply bid the spirits a temporary farewell. Leave your altar, allowing the candles and incense to burn through the night. In the morning, dispose of any leftover offerings responsibly.

Feasts

At this point, we are well-acquainted with the importance of food in the festival of Samhain. It should come as no surprise then that one of the most important and most popular Samhain rituals is structured around food.

During the sabbat, many people perform rituals known as 'dumb suppers,' also called 'ancestor feasts' (Kolirin, 2022). We have already learned a great deal about these types of ancestrally-oriented meals, but they bear going into some more. Before you begin cooking and baking all of the dishes you wish to lay out on your ritual table, begin your preparations with decorations. No Samhain feast table must be used bare. Many people choose to decorate the tables at which they will feast similarly to their ancestral altars. On your table, you can place talismans of your ancestors, as well as any other plants, crystals, sigils, or iconography that you feel will strengthen your connection to them. If you prefer something more understated, decorate the table in the colors of death (black and white), while maybe even weaving in some autumnal colors to truly bring your table full circle as the setting for a Samhain feast.

Moving on to the star of the show, the food, it is important to keep your ancestors in mind when preparing your courses. More specifically, keep the ancestors you are trying to contact in mind. Focus on the dishes they favored when they were alive, as well as those which held some meaning for them, whether personally, culturally, or because they formed part of their own Samhain feasts in the past. Prepare these dishes as close as possible to the actual supper, as their effect will be more powerful (and more respectful) if they are presented fresh.

When the feast arrives, set the table, designating the seat at the top of the table as the place for the ancestors. Even if you are honoring multiple ancestors with one ritual, set only one place for their spirits. Once everyone is seated, the supper begins with you offering up a plate of the prepared food for the ancestors. Set the plate on their place and invite them to join you for the meal. After this, the dumb supper is in full effect, and there must be total silence for the duration of the meal. Traditionally, a bell was used to signal the imposition and lifting of silence. If bells aren't to your taste, arrange with your guests to acknowledge the feast as begun once the offering is made. Ensure that you also inform them of the end of the dumb supper, which can be announced by clearing the place set for the ancestors. Between these two actions, however, the meal must be eaten in complete silence. Once you have ended the ritual, and thanked the ancestors for their presence, you and your guests may finish the rest of your meal, but you needn't be silent anymore. Should you feel that the act of presenting the ancestors with an offering is not enough to celebrate them, do the following: once you have ended the silent supper, but before you have bid farewell to the ancestral spirits, go around the table and ask each guest to share a memory or story of the ancestor(s) being honored (these can be prepared beforehand). When the last guest has shared, thank the ancestors, remind them of their impact in your lives, and send them on their way.

Natural Connection

Samhain cannot be separated from the natural world. The festival originated as a celebration of nature's gifts, and so many of these gifts are still used in modern-day Samhain and Halloween festivities. Given this deep connection, an excellent (and easy) way to enjoy a Samhain ritual is by spending some time outside during the sabbat.

The easiest way to connect to nature is to simply *be* in it. On the night of Samhain, go for a walk and drink in the color, texture, and energy of every plant and animal you come across. If you would like to take your stroll up a supernatural notch, try to find a hawthorn tree, and spend some time under its branches in the moonlight. It is said that creatures like fairies may be found near these trees on Samhain night. Even if you find none, the exploration allows you to spend the evening basking in the light of a Samhain moon.

Another outdoor ritual you can execute during Samhain is one of the oldest performed during a festival: a bonfire. Assuming that the area in which you are holding your celebration allows for it, gather your friends and family and light a fire to mark the end of the year. To add another element of ritualistic flavor, when gathered around the bonfire, have each person write on a piece of paper the things they want to leave in the year that ends on Samhain. One by one, toss the papers into the fire and feel yourselves letting go of the past.

So much of Samhain can be enjoyed in the great outdoors. If you are casting spells or decorating for the sabbat, try to see where it would be possible to move your activities outside. Nature is the common thread that runs through all of us, the spirits of the Otherworld, and even through the sabbat itself. Commune with the natural world, if only to open your eyes to all the wonders it will perform on this holy night.

Key Takeaways

- Rituals form an extremely important part of Samhain, providing people with the best and most accessible way to celebrate the sabbat.

- Ancestral rituals most often take shape as séances in which practitioners attempt to establish and maintain a connection with the spirits of the dead. Common Samhain séances involve entering the Otherworld and communicating directly with the spirits found there.

- Alternatively, Samhain séances can also involve communing and establishing a relationship with the spirits in your immediate surroundings.

- Ancestral feasts, also known as dumb suppers, are a ritualistic means to bring people together to celebrate the lives of those who they have loved and lost.

- Samhain may also be observed by spending time in nature and connecting with the ancient roots of the festival.

- By taking a walk outside, lighting a bonfire or integrating time spent outdoors into the execution of other festivities, celebrators are able to become more attuned with the natural world. This, in turn, will enable them to understand the sabbat and its basic tenets more deeply.

CHAPTER 9:

The Next Cycle

> *At Samhain, we cast off the old year's attachments and turn our attention to the coming scarcity of winter. We feast on the last of the summer's bounty. We contemplate what is worth saving and nurturing during the dark of winter. We try to make friends with Death.* –Michelle Gruben

Although Samhain is perhaps the best-known of the sabbats that make up the Wheel of the Year, it is not the only holy day that is observed. In fact, there are seven other sabbats that Wiccans, Neo-Pagans, and people from an array of other spiritual groups honor during each annual cycle. We conclude this book by examining the ways in which Samhain is connected to the next sabbat in the Wheel of the Year, as well as how you can move from celebrating Samhain to the winter festival.

Beginning Anew

Once Samhain has passed, we find ourselves in a new year, with the potential for very many new beginnings. We also find ourselves in the dark part of the year, with the last vestiges of autumnal warmth fading soon after the sabbat has ended. As the festival that marks the beginning of a new year, Samhain effectively sets the entire Wheel of the Year in motion, and brings the light part of the year to a close. In the dark winter that follows, another sabbat is observed: Yule.

More popularly known as the winter solstice, Yule marks the midwinter, placing us equidistant from the autumn and the spring. Alternatively, Yule marks the halfway point between Samhain and Imbolc. Though the two seasonal festivals differ somewhat, with Samhain including harvest celebrations and Yule serving as the catalyst for the season of the harvest yet to come (Mark, 2019), we can take some aspects of the former's festivities and use them to build those we will undertake during the latter.

When Yule comes around, we are far enough into the new year that we can take stock of what we have achieved so far. Review your Samhain intentions at midwinter and see how your plans for the new cycle are coming along. If you have cast spells that are intended to take effect over the entire annum, check up on their progress and see what you can do to strengthen their effects if you feel they have faded somewhat.

Yule is the first sabbat of the new year, and is also more of an individual celebration. Group celebrations do take place, but tend to be smaller. As such, find some time after Samhain to coordinate your plans with the people in your life, allowing yourself enough time to gather materials for either individual or group rituals and spells.

Yule is an entirely seasonal sabbat, celebrating the winter and helping us to prepare for the light part of the year that is on the way. Revel in the darkness of Samhain, and carry this darkness through to you with Yule, but be sure to leave room for the light to return once more.

Key Takeaways

- Samhain, the New Year, is followed by Yule, the festival of midwinter.

- Yule celebrations are more individual, differing from those of Samhain in that they celebrate the darkness but also begin preparing for the light of the approaching spring.

- When moving from Samhain to Yule, it would be advisable to determine whether you will be celebrating on your own or in a group, as you will need to plan rituals and spells accordingly.

Conclusion

Samhain therefore marks the beginning of darkness, and thus the beginning of life, a time for "The Gathering" of all beings. –Brendan Mac Gonagle

The festival of Samhain is incredibly multi-faceted–so much so that it can often be overwhelming to know what exactly it is that we must understand about the sabbat. Despite this difficulty, the festival can be encapsulated in one sentence: Samhain is a time of beginnings and endings, a time that we look toward life to celebrate it, and toward death to honor it.

If you would like a more expansive summary, it bears repeating here that Samhain began as an Ancient Celtic festival celebrated by Pagans and Druids alike, one in which fire played an enormously important role as it served as catalyst for the entire festival. As the centuries wore on and Christian missionaries arrived on Celtic shores, the harvest and New Year's festival took on a more ancestral aspect. This ancestral reverence increased, until the Catholic Church eventually invented their own holidays during Samhain. Though certainly undesired at the time, today we celebrate Samhain, Halloween, and the modern evolutions of the Christian holidays side-by-side.

What makes Samhain such a distinct festival is that it exists in many different iterations around the world. Though many of these festivals predate the Celtic celebrations, their survival demonstrates the fact that seasonal celebrations and the honoring of one's ancestors is a universal practice. Festivals like Día de los Muertos, the Blessed Easter, Akwasidae and Awukudae, Wag, Obon, Chuseok, and the Hungry Ghost Festival all remind us that cultures, regardless of how fundamentally different they are, will always place great importance on the lives of those who came before, as we not only learn from them but are guided by them as we make our way through life.

Samhain exists in many forms today, and whether you approach it from the perspective of a Neo-Pagan, Neo-Druid, Wiccan, Christian, or even a candy-focused costume-wearer, the sabbat exists for everyone. Celebrations bring people together and allow us to look back and recognize the influence the past has on us. Whether you are sitting down to a dumb supper, providing ancestral offerings at your altar, or casting a spell asking for their help and guidance, the forces of time gone by make an appearance in every form of celebration.

Darkness is very closely associated with Samhain, and the act of communing with the entities of the Otherworld and welcoming the darkened winter may seem intimidating to some. If you count yourself among those who feel a little bit of fear when they think of Samhain, I would like to remind you that you are only aware of the darkness because there is light in your life. When celebrating the sabbat, lean into this light as it manifests in your beliefs, your family, and your friends. Embrace the light, as it will help illuminate the darkness, and as terrifying as the shadows may seem, you'll find that there is so much to learn and love there—you need only take the first step.

Thank You

I would like to extend my sinccrest gratitude to you for purchasing this book.

If you enjoyed your reading experience, please leave a review. Your feedback not only lets others know what you think of the book, but also helps me to know which topics you would like to explore next.

Should you be interested, be sure to check out some of the other titles available for purchase:

- *Soul Retrieval: Restore Energy and Vitality by Healing Trauma from Soul Loss*

- *Energy Space Clearing: Restore Positivity and Harmony in Everyday Spaces*

- Wheel of the Year Series. This series comprises eight (8) books in total, each exploring one of the eight different sabbats that make up the Wheel of the Year.

About the Author

Laura Garcia was born and raised in the American South, where she lives with her husband and two daughters. Her hobbies include reading and cooking delicious meals. Additionally, Laura harbors a fierce passion for spiritual truths, which she pursues through the exploration of various religious texts and constructs, as well as through the implementation of reality-creation techniques. Hence her interest in gaining spiritual so as to understand the nature of reality and the ways in which life may be lived to its fullest.

References

2spirits. (2022, December 7). *Best money spells for wealth and abundance*. 2Spirits. https://www.2spirits.com/best-money-spells

Adae Kese festival. (2012). Travel to Discover Ghana. Www.travel-To-Discover-

Ghana.com. http://www.travel-to-discover-ghana.com/adae-kese-festival.html

Adae Kese festival. (2021). Beyond the Return. https://beyondthereturn.org/adae-kese/

Aidoo, K. (2018, June 13). *Celebrating Akiwasidae with the Ashanti people of Kumasi,*

Ghana. Culture Trip. https://theculturetrip.com/africa/ghana/articles/celebrating-akiwasidae-with-the-ashanti-people-of-kumasi-ghana/

The Akwasidae festival of Ghana's Ashanti Kingdom that celebrates powerful Golden

Stool brought down from heaven. (2022, April 23). GhanaWeb. https://www.ghanaweb.com/GhanaHomePage/NewsArchive/The-Akwasidae-festival-of-Ghana-s-Ashanti-Kingdom-that-celebrates-powerful-Golden-Stool-brought-down-from-heaven-1522220

Albot, N. (2021, April 15). *Easter traditions in Moldova–Eat like Moldovans.* Eat like Moldovans. https://eatlikemoldovans.com/easter-traditions-in-moldova/

Amgborale Blay, Y. (2014, August 16). *Adae | Akan festival.* Encyclopedia Britannica. https://www.britannica.com/topic/Adae

Anuwen, R. (2021, April 26). *Beltane Blessings and Making Spell Jars.* Kindred Spirit Magazine. https://kindredspirit.co.uk/2021/04/26/beltane-blessings-and-making-spell-jars/

Arizona-Sonora Desert Museum. (n.d.). *Dia de los Muertos Background Information.* Www.desertmuseum.org. https://www.desertmuseum.org/visit/noche2.php

Basile, L. M. (2021, March 1). An 11-line poetry spell for healing. *Luna Luna Magazine.* http://www.lunalunamagazine.com/dark/spell-poetry-healing

The best crystals for Samhain. (2022, October 22). New Moon Beginnings. https://newmoonbeginnings.com/best-crystals-for-samhain/

Bhagat, D. (2018, October 30). *The origins and practices of: Samhain, Día de los Muertos, and All Saints Day.* Bpl.org. https://www.bpl.org/blogs/post/the-origins-and-practices-of-holidays-samhain-dia-de-los-muertos-and-all-saints-day/

Bios Urn. (2017, October 25). *Festivals that honor the dead all around the world.* https://urnabios.com/festivals-that-honor-the-dead-around-world/

Birch, J. (2022). *Praying through the Celtic year–Samhain.* Www.faithandworship.com. https://www.faithandworship.com/Samhain_praying_though_the_Celtic_year.htm

Bishop, J. (2019, November 17). *Who are the Neo-Druids and What do They Believe?*

Bishop's Encyclopedia of Religion, Society and Philosophy. https://jamesbishopblog.com/2019/11/17/who-are-the-Neo-Druids-and-what-do-they-believe/

Blessed Easter (Pashtele Blajinilor). (2023). Prospect.md.

https://www.prospect.md/en/holidays/blessed-easter-pashtele-blajinilor.html

Booth, J. (2018, October 29). 7 crystals for Halloween 2018 to help you harness all that spooky energy for good. *Bustle.* https://www.bustle.com/p/7-crystals-for-halloween-2018-to-help-you-harness-all-that-spooky-energy-for-good-13017040

Brown, M. (2022, December 8). *LibGuides: Samhain: The Celtic origins of Halloween*. Westportlibrary.libguides.com. https://westportlibrary.libguides.com/Samhain

Campbell, R. (2021, November 24). *The spiritual significance of Samhain*. Rebecca Campbell. https://rebeccacampbell.me/create-a-samhain-altar/

Centre of Excellence. (2021, December 30). *New year spells for guidance and to rejuvenate your spiritual purpose for 2022*. Centre of Excellence. Www.centreofexcellence.com. https://www.centreofexcellence.com/spells-for-guidance/

Clan Campbell Society. (n.d.). *Samhain, Halloween, and the Day of the Dead*. Clan

Campbell. https://www.ccsna.org/samhain-halloween-and-the-day-of-the-dead

Clowes, M. M. (2016, October 13). *Manifesting spells*. https://www.academia.edu/33877999/Collaborative_Spell_for_Samhain_Weekend_2016_SOUL_CAKES_FOR_SAMHAIN_The_Guided_Tarot_for_The_Celtic_Witches_Clan_manifesting_spelss

Coughlin, S. (2018, October 30). *5 Samhain rituals you can perform for Halloween*. Www.refinery29.com. https://www.refinery29.com/en-us/samhain-Pagan-rituals

De Souza Soares, A. L. (2013). *Samhain ao Halloween: Da festividade céltica a comemoraçãoamericana.* https://www.academia.edu/4723924/Do_Samhain_ao_Halloween_Samhain_to_Halloween_From_the_Celtic_Feast_to_the_American_Celebration_

do Nascimento, C. (2020, October 30). *Celebrating Samhain: How to set up the best altar and perform the right rituals.* Www.kelleemaize.com. https://www.kelleemaize.com/post/celebrating-samhain-how-to-set-up-the-best-altar-and-perform-the-right-rituals

Dorvlo, D. (2020, September 30). *Celebrating Adae (Akwasidae) festival | BreathList.* Breathlist.com. https://breathlist.com/africa/ghana/culture-and-people/celebrating-adae-akwasidae-festival/

Evert Hopman, E. (2021). *Celebrating Samhain with plants.* Www.innertraditions.com. https://www.innertraditions.com/blog/celebrating-samhain-with-plants

Festival of the Wag. (n.d.). Historyofegypt.net. Retrieved January 14, 2023, from https://historyofegypt.net/?page_id=980

Fields, K. (2022, July 5). *20 Samhain herbs & crystals for your autumn spells & rituals.* Otherworldly Oracle. https://otherworldlyoracle.com/samhain-herbs-crystals/

Foley, M., & O'Donnell, H. (2009). *Treat or trick? : Halloween in a globalising world.* Cambridge Scholars Publishing.

Fox, S. (2019). *Celebrating Samhain*. Circle Sanctuary. https://www.circlesanctuary.org/index.php/celebrating-the-seasons/celebrating-samhain

Gabriel, A. (2021, October 30). *The Pagan and Christian origins of Halloween*. FOX Weather. https://www.foxweather.com/lifestyle/the-Pagan-and-christian-origins-of-halloween-samhain

Geiling, N. (2014, October 30). *Festivals of the Dead Around the World*. Smithsonian Magazine. https://www.smithsonianmag.com/travel/festivals-dead-around-world-180953160/

Gruben, M. (2022, September 30). *Create an ancestor altar for Samhain: 7 easy ways to celebrate your honored dead*. Grove and Grotto. https://www.groveandgrotto.com/blogs/articles/create-an-ancestor-altar-for-samhain-7-easy-ways-to-celebrate-your-honored-dead

Hawthorn & Honey. (2021, August 26). *Samhain rituals and the thinning of the veil*. Hawthorn & Honey. https://www.hawthornandhoney.com/journal/samhain-rituals

History.com Editors. (2018a, April 6). *Samhain*. HISTORY. https://www.history.com/topics/holidays/samhain

History.com Editors. (2018b, October 30). *Day of the dead*. History; A&E Television Networks. https://www.history.com/topics/halloween/day-of-the-dead

How to set up a gorgeous Samhain altar. (2021, October 4). The Goddess Lifestyle Plan®

https://www.goddesslifestyleplan.com/set-gorgeous-samhain-altar/

Jr, D. T. M. (2014, October 31). *"Pangangaluluwa": Reviving a dying custom.* INQUIRER.net. https://newsinfo.inquirer.net/647988/pangangaluluwa-reviving-a-dying-custom

Kiger, P. J. (2020, October 27). *How the early Catholic church christianized Halloween.* HISTORY. https://www.history.com/news/halloween-samhain-celts-catholic-church

Kolirin, L. (2022, October 28). *Samhain: How Pagans celebrate the darkness.* Religion Media Centre. https://religionmediacentre.org.uk/news/samhain-how-Pagans-celebrate-the-darkness/

Kozocarl, J., Owens, Y., & North, J. (1995). *The witch's book of days.* Beach Holme Publishing Ltd. (Original work published 1995)

Lang, C. (2018, October 30). What Is Samhain? What to Know About the Ancient Pagan Festival That Came Before Halloween. *Time.* Time. https://time.com/5434659/halloween-Pagan-origins-in-samhain/

Leonardi, L. (2020). *Plants to know on all Hallows Eve.* Opus Grows. Opusgrows.com. https://opusgrows.com/blogs/journal/plants-to-know-on-all-hallows-eve

lizleafloor. (2020, October 28). *Crossing the veil: The pre-Christian origins of Halloween and Samhain*. Ancient Origins Reconstructing the Story of Humanity's Past. https://www.ancient-origins.net/myths-legends-europe/origins-halloween-samhain-002271

Lotti, L., & Primrose. (2018, October 29). *Celebrating Samhain and helpful herbs*. Primrose. https://www.primrose.co.uk/blog/celebrations-and-holidays/celebrating-samhain-and-helpful-herbs/

Mac Gonagle, B. (2016). Samhain–Some Reflections on the Celtic Origins of Halloween. https://www.academia.edu/29430953/SAMHAIN_Some_Reflections_on_the_Celtic_Origins_of_Halloween

Mac Gonagle, B. (2017). Samonos/Samhain/Halloween–On the Celtic festival of the (not quite) dead. https://www.academia.edu/34915810/SAMONOS_SAMHAIN_HALLOWEEN_ON_THE_CELTIC_FESTIVAL_OF_THE_NOT_QUITE_DEAD

Madara, M. (2018, October 31). Rituals to fully embrace the Samhain season. *Luna Luna Magazine*. http://www.lunalunamagazine.com/dark/rituals-for-samhain

Mahollitz, E. (2021, October 20). *Honoring Samhain*. Meagan Rose Wilson–Holistic Parenting Resources. https://meaganrosewilson.com/2021/10/samhain/

The magic of new year. (2020, December 3). Smells like Spells. Smellslikespells.com. https://smellslikespells.com/the-magic-of-new-year/

Mark, J. (2017, March 17). *Festivals in ancient Egypt.* World History Encyclopedia. https://www.worldhistory.org/article/1032/festivals-in-ancient-egypt/

Mark, J. J. (2019, January 28). *Wheel of the Year.* World History Encyclopedia. https://www.worldhistory.org/Wheel_of_the_Year/

Matovich, J. (2020, October 16). *The lazy witch: 5 simple spells and rituals to celebrate Samhain.* Jodi Matovich. https://jodimatovich.com/new-blog/thelazywitch

McConnell, H. (2020, October 25). *Best crystals for Samhain.* My Dream Crystals. https://www.mydreamcrystals.com/blog/best-crystals-for-samhain/

McGarry, M. (2019, October 30). *A guide to Irish Halloween magic spells.* Www.rte.ie. https://www.rte.ie/brainstorm/2019/1016/1083781-a-guide-to-irish-halloween-magic-spells/

McGrade, G. (2022, October 24). *8 ways to celebrate Samhain, AKA the Witches' New Year.* Dazed. https://www.dazeddigital.com/beauty/article/57205/1/ways-to-celebrate-samhain-Pagan-halloween-witches-new-year

Merrill, C. (2020, October 28). The rituals of Samhain. *Claudia Merrill*. https://www.claudiamerrill.com/blog/the-rituals-of-samhain

Neshevich, V. (2020, October 28). *Five important crystals for Samhain*. Green Moon Apothecary Ltd. https://greenmoon.ca/blogs/blog/five-important-crystals-for-samhain

OBOD. (2019, December 15). *Samhain Festival*. Order of Bards, Ovates and Druids. https://Druidry.org/druid-way/teaching-and-practice/druid-festivals/samhain-festival

Pearcy, C. (2022, August 3). *Seven crystals for Samhain*. Exemplore. https://exemplore.com/Paganism/Seven-Crystals-for-Samhain

Penguin Travel. (2018, July 29). *The Akwasidae Festival in Ghana*. Penguin Travel. https://www.penguintravel.com/New/438/0/TheAkwasidaeFestivalinGhana.html

Pocu, K. (2022). Adae Kese Festival–Asante Kingdom Great Festival. *Mr. Pocu Blog*. https://mrpocu.com/adae-kese-festival-asante-kingdom-great-festival/

Pomeni (Moldova). (2022, September 5). Global Informality Project. Www.in Formality.com. https://www.in-formality.com/wiki/index.php?title=Pomeni_(Moldova)

Rafaniello, M. (2020). *Akwasidae festival*. Mondo Internazionale. https://mondointernazionale.com/en/culturalmenteimparando/festa-akwasidae

Rattray, R. S. (n.d.). *The Adae Kese festival*. Africanpoems.net. Retrieved January 14, 2023, from https://africanpoems.net/gods-ancestors/the-adae-kese-festival/

Regan, S. (2022, February 2). *Love, money & more: This tool will help you fulfill your innermost desires*. Mindbodygreen. https://www.mindbodygreen.com/articles/spell-jars

Renée, J. (2008, December 10). *Candle spell to welcome the new year*. Llewellyn Worldwide. https://www.llewellyn.com/journal/article/1772

Samhain. (n.d.). The Druid Network. Retrieved January 14, 2023, from https://druidnetwork.org/what-is-Druidry/rites-and-rituals/rites-celebrate-seasonal-festivals/samhain/

Samhain: 12+ rituals, traditions, & easy ways to celebrate. (2022, October 5). Tea & Rosemary. https://teaandrosemary.com/samhain-rituals-traditions-ways-to-celebrate/

Samahin, lord of darkness. (n.d.). Holiday Insights. Www.holidayinsights.com. https://www.holidayinsights.com/halloween/samhain.htm

Samhain rituals and traditions. (2017). *Pagan Holiday Rituals and Traditions*. We'Moon. https://wemoon.ws/blogs/Pagan-holiday-traditions/samhain

Sherman, E. (2020, October 23). *How to celebrate Wiccan Samhain instead of Halloween this year*. Matador Network.

https://matadornetwork.com/read/celebrate-wiccan-samhain-instead-halloween-year/

Smith, I. (2019, September 18). *Setting up and decorating your Samhain altar*. Witchbox. https://witchbox.co.uk/blogs/witchbox-blog/samhain-altar

Soulful Samhain. (2018, October 30). Dragon Herbarium. https://dragonherbarium.com/blogs/blog/soulful-samhain

Stewart, T. (2018, October 7). *6 crystals for Samhain or Halloween–The witch of Lupine Hollow*. The Witch of Lupine Hollow. https://witchoflupinehollow.com/2018/10/07/6-crystals-for-samhain-or-halloween/

Sutcliffe, A. (2014, July). *Samhain ritual*. The Druid Network. https://druidnetwork.org/what-is-Druidry/rites-and-rituals/rites-celebrate-seasonal-festivals/samhain/samhain-ritual/

Team, A. A. S. (2021, October 25). *Halloween in other cultures and languages*. Ad Astra, Inc. https://ad-astrainc.com/2021/10/halloween-in-other-cultures-and-languages/

Tremeer, E. (2021, October 25). *How to celebrate Samhain 2021: rituals, spells, tarot spreads, and more...* Liminal 11. https://liminal11.com/2021/10/25/how-to-celebrate-samhain-2020-rituals-spells-tarot-spreads-and-more/

Ventures, C. (2019). *Day of the Dead (Dia De Los Muertos)*. Day of the Dead. https://dayofthedead.holiday/

WAG: *Egyptian Festival of the Dead*. (2022, August 4). Celebrate Pagan Holidays. https://www.celebratePaganholidays.com/summer/wag-egyptian-festival-of-the-dead

Ward, K. (2021, August 23). Want even more Halloween? Here's how to celebrate Samhain, aka the Witches' New Year. *Cosmopolitan.* https://www.cosmopolitan.com/lifestyle/a34360772/samhain-traditions/

Weaving, M. (2020, October 8). *Samhain solo ritual.* Order of Bards, Ovates and Druids. https://Druidry.org/resources/samhain-solo-ritual

Weiss, G. (2015, October 28). This Halloween season, real-life witches share spells for money, confidence and success. *Entrepreneur.* https://www.entrepreneur.com/leadership/this-halloween-season-real-life-witches-share-spells-for/252040

What is Samhain? The History of The Pagan Celebration. (2020, October 20). Sea Witch Botanicals. https://seawitchbotanicals.com/blogs/swb/what-is-samhain-the-history-of-the-Pagan-celebration

Wigington, P. (2019, August 14). *7 sacred plants for the Samhain season.* Learn Religions. https://www.learnreligions.com/sacred-plants-of-the-samhain-sabbat-3879864

Wigington, P. (2020, April 29). *Set up your altar for the Samhain sabbat*. Learn Religions. https://www.learnreligions.com/setting-up-a-samhain-altar-2562711

Willowroot, A. (2003, December 31). *Spell: New Year's Eve ritual*. Llewellyn Worldwide. https://www.llewellyn.com/spell.php?spell_id=1320

Wood, C. (2021, October 21). *3 Types of simple Samhain rituals*. Www.corinnawood.com. https://www.corinnawood.com/blog/samhain-rituals

Woolsey, B. (2022, October 24). *The disappearing Philippine tradition of "souling" for rice cakes*. Atlas Obscura. https://www.atlasobscura.com/articles/philippine-halloween-traditions

Printed in Great Britain
by Amazon